MUSIC & FLOWERS

Growing up on Clydeside in the 30s and 40s

Anna Rosalind Hutchison

Thistleburr Publishing
www.thistleburrpublishing.co.uk

MUSIC & FLOWERS

Growing up on Clydeside in the 30s and 40s

Copyright © Anna Rosalind Hutchison, 2018

Thistleburr Publishing

ISBN- 978-1-9164684-0-5

Publisher's Note: Some names and identifying details have been changed to protect the privacy of individuals.

All images copyright the author except:

When Time, who steals our years away

Shall steal our pleasures too

The memory of the past shalt stay

And half our joys renew

—Thomas More

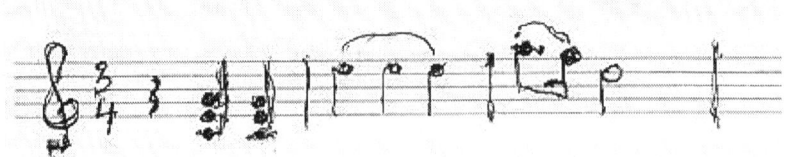

GIFFNOCK

George V was on the throne and Ramsay MacDonald in number 10 Downing Street at the head of a Labour government, when I was born towards the end of 1930. That same year Amy Johnson, in her 'Gypsy Moth', had made her solo flight to Australia, sliced bread – the wonder loaf – had been launched onto the domestic market, and the St Kildans were finally evacuated from their remote island, thus saying a final farewell to their unique way of life. The decade before had seen recovery from the Great War, the launch of the League of Nations, independence from Britain for the Irish Free State, and the crippling general strike of 1926. For the young and those that had the means the decade was the time to enjoy life again, with the war behind them, and it became known for its partying flappers and the arrival of the Charleston and swing music from the States. The Wall Street crash of 1929 had repercussions around the world, with much resulting poverty and hardship, even close to home. Stalin's reign of terror had begun in Russia and Fascism was on the rise in Germany and Italy. The storm clouds were already bubbling up over Europe only twelve short years after the end of the war that was meant "to end all wars".

But of course I knew nothing of all this until much later when some of it was absorbed as modern history. I was fortunate to be born into a well-educated, middle class family, and a secure environment. My father was in the teaching profession, as my mother had been too until her marriage. He had a secure job, unlike so many men at a time of high unemployment, especially in industrial areas such as neighbouring Glasgow.

At home there was already a family of growing boys who must have felt their routine environment sadly disrupted by the arrival of a baby, and a girl at that. I was later told that Andrew, into his senior school days had, on the day following my birth, replied enthusiastically, "Oui, monsieur" to his French master's enquiry, "have you got a sister, Hutchison?"

David was more doubtful and, after several days of questioning as to whether he had told his news to his school pals, he eventually said, "I've told Kenny but he's promised not to spread it."

The family before my arrival.

Our home in Giffnock was a semidetached, stone-fronted bungalow which had been built during the housing boom following the war. Well into the 19th century, Giffnock had been an area of farmland and moorland but by the 1850s several large houses and estates had been established. Some industry had developed and a railway line running into the city had been laid. The limestone quarries at Giffnock had produced a lovely stone, much of which was used in the building of Victorian Glasgow. After that, Giffnock kept expanding from a quiet country village into a huge area of suburbia.

Birthplace at Giffnock.

Our garden backed onto the outer edge of the estate of Eastwood, home to Lord Weir, the Glasgow industrialist. The woodland here was a perfect fairyland to a small child, once able to climb the fence. I slashed my leg badly on the fence one day when I was quite small and called it "bad" wire for several years till I discovered that, bad as it might be, it was really "barbed". In springtime I picked bunches of bluebells here from a haze of misty blue that stretched as far as the eye could see. David, as a small boy, had picked bunches of primroses and wood anemones here for his mother, calling them "wooden enemies". This was private land of course and I didn't dare venture too far. My brothers and their friends had been more adventurous, and had even covered hollows with brushwood in the hope that the estate gamekeeper might fall into their traps.

Bluebells.

Wood anemone.

The garden was a good sized one and probably typical of the 1930s. The greenhouse allowed my mother to grow lots of lovely plants. There were Calceolarias, Schizanthus (the poor man's orchid), and Cinerarias, the last, when potted up gave winter colour in the house. It was heated by a coal boiler and its large pipes I once hoped would hide me from the dentist visiting to extract teeth from my brother David and I heard him screaming! These were the days when both family doctor and dentist would come to you rather than you going to them. But of course such services had to be paid for.

At the top of the garden there was a solid brick-based garden shed which made a wonderful place for a little girl to play with friends. There we had dollies' tea parties with small real bone china cups and saucers, and teapot. Leaves and stones, and bits and pieces from the garden served as cakes and biscuits. The shed, with its warm woody smell, housed all the garden tools – spades and forks, Dutch hoe and lawnmower, riddles, watering cans, twine, brass sprayer, daisy lifter, and much more. Here were deck chairs gaudily striped in many colours, and the summer swing seat with its coloured canvas shade for the hottest of days.

Typical of the time, the plot nearest to the house was planted with hybrid tea roses, under-planted with wallflowers and forget-me-nots in spring, and I seem to remember edged in places with Auriculas (dusty millers), a plant beloved by the Victorians. Another large plot was given over to the cultivation of Chrysanthemums, my mother's pride and joy. She lavished much attention and care on these and had such success with them that, in season, visitors departed with large bunches, still leaving plenty for display in the house vases. With their spicy smell they came in all colours, yellows, bronze, pinks, mauves and white, small and large. One of my earliest memories, possibly the earliest for I must have been only around one year old and still not speaking, was being held in my mother's arms to admire a bunch of chrysanthemums and repeating 'F-F-F' in delight! Was this an early indication of my lifelong love affair with plants I wonder?

Chrysanthemums painted by Aunt Chris.

Before I was five, a small patch at the end of the rose bed had been allocated to me, where I grew double daisies and scattered annuals from seed packets that would have cost next to nothing in these days. A little fork and trowel, and a small watering can crowned my delight. Elsewhere in the garden were more flowers I certainly couldn't name, some vegetables and fruit, and a top area of grass where I learnt to make daisy chains. Rambler roses hugged a side fence and winter jasmine with its starry yellow flowers, clung to the back wall of the house. The front garden was given over largely to a rockery which I am sure was typical of the times, and in spring it was a riot of colour with mats of saxifrages and candy tuft, exuberant clouds of Aubretia, and the blazing yellow of Alyssum. One day I was thrilled to find a toad half-hidden under one of the stones. Toads, like frogs, require water for spawning and that was not far away. Otherwise they spread out and are territorial, this one having chosen us! The ground opposite had been open as my brothers grew up, leading down to the burn. They had gone bird nesting there and I remember David had a small collection of birds' eggs. Now more houses were being built opposite us. The march of development had begun, never to cease in my lifetime.

On wet days there was the attic to play in. The rafters smelt warm and woody and I was cosy here as the rain drummed on the roof window. As with most attics it was cluttered with suitcases and trunks, skates, tennis rackets, golf clubs, and my father's old kit bag and army cap from his days as a lieutenant in the Royal Artillery.

A battered old rocking horse here had been much loved by my brothers. Now their Hornby train set was laid out on the floor with its tracks, signal box, and locomotives. Dahlia tubers were stored here in wooden trays over winter and a spare bed allowed me to play nursemaid to some of my dolls and indulge in a world of make-believe. Being a little girl, of course, I wanted to help with household chores. There had been a maid when I was tiny, but the hardships of the Depression meant that most households had to make savings. Now there remained only a char to help with the rough work.

Daddy in uniform, Great War.

Although my father was in a safe profession, he, like other public servants had in the early 30s had to accept a ten percent pay cut. This made him in later life critical of those who believed constant pay rises were theirs by right. He could sometimes be rather intolerant and certainly didn't suffer fools gladly. In later years I recognised him as having a somewhat hard exterior but with a warm, soft centre. On Saturday mornings he would allow me to creep into bed with him where he would tell me made-up stories about naughty teddy bears climbing trees and dropping nuts onto the park ranger below, and getting up to many other pranks.

Saturday was park day. Contrary to the fashion of the time he was not ashamed to be seen pushing me along to Rouken Glen in my pushchair. Such days are among my earliest memories, either being pushed or walking a little on slightly muddy Rhododendron-lined paths and looking down on the Auldhouse burn with its fine waterfall. Sometimes there were ducks along the burn-side. Rouken Glen estate had over its history several different names and owners but in the early 20th century it was finally gifted to the city of Glasgow by Lord Rowallan.

The park's boating pond was constructed around 1924. My brothers often took out little pleasure boats here and sailed around carefree. In hard winters, if there was a sufficient depth of ice, skating was allowed and they took advantage of this too until old enough to take their skates to the Crossmyloof indoor rink. Before I might have emulated them we were on the point of leaving Giffnock for a very different life in the west end of Glasgow. And my time with boats was yet to come!

David, Barrie & Ian at Rouken Glen.

Wash days at home were exciting as I stood on a stool at the sink, sloshing about up to my elbows in hot soapy water. As usual back then the kitchen had a sink where dishes were washed up and vegetables prepared, and alongside a deep tub where clothes were soaked and rubbed up and down on a corrugated, wooden framed scrubbing board before being rinsed. Then they were pushed through the mangle which was fixed with screw clamps between the sink and the tub, ready to hang out to dry on the top grass. Whites were boiled in a large container on the top of the gas cooker, and some items had to be starched. Men's collars at that time were often separate to shirts and had to be stiff to be smart and white tablecloths and napkins were the norm, certainly if there were guests. Robin starch was a necessary wash day item. A laundry van called weekly to collect large items and to return the previous lot.

Spring cleaning was quite an upheaval. Everything was cleaned. Carpets, not fitted in those days, were taken out to the clothes lines and beaten hard with a wicker carpet beater. The surrounds, whether of wood or lino were washed and polished. Furniture was moved, washed with water and vinegar, and then polished. Curtains were taken down to be washed or sent to the cleaners. Mirrors and pictures – all cleaned. I remember during the war damp bread was used to clean the wallpapers, and when the carpets were re-laid they were always turned to even out the wear. Coal fires meant a lot of work, but they were lovely to sit at and see pictures in the glowing embers and one of the loveliest things in winter was to toast bread or muffins at the fire on the end of a long brass toasting fork.

The kitchen of the 1930s was basic with no washing machine or refrigerator or fancy gadgets. At one end we had a coal cellar with access both from inside and out, and a shelved larder with an open grill to allow circulation of air. Milk was delivered daily in bottles left on the doorstep by the milkman who did his rounds in his milk float. More than once he took me and a school friend on some of his rounds. No panic in the family about this as there would be now and no ban on accepting the odd sweetie from an old man in the park! In fact I was told later that as a small girl I often wanted to speak to older men. Possibly I thought they would all be as kind and gentle as my Daddy.

Message boys on bicycles regularly delivered goods from the local grocers and on Saturdays there were always three bars of Cadbury's chocolate for me and my brothers. Two other people made regular, if infrequent calls at the back door. One was the Onion Johnnie, always in his beret, who arrived with magnificent strings of onions on the handlebars of his bicycle, all the way from Brittany I think. The other was a turbaned and bearded gentleman with a bulging leather suitcase stuffed full of all manner of cloths, dusters, brushes, and knick-knacks – I thought he was a bit scary.

Often I accompanied Mummy to Eastwood Toll for shopping. This was most fun in autumn when I could kick my way through drifts of fallen leaves looking forward to being given a couple of biscuits for "being a good girl" in the local bakers shop, A.F. Reid's. Many biscuits at that time were not packaged in any way and were displayed loose in glass topped tins. My favourites were like the café noir ones the adults ate but were iced in different colours and depicted different animals of one sort or another on the top.

The shops here replaced the old Toll House, long gone, but at one time it lay at an important crossroads linking Glasgow to the south and Paisley to the east. But the crossroads was still called the Toll. Another group of shops lay perhaps half a mile along the main road towards the city. Here I sometimes watched cheese being cut by a wire onto a wooden board, then weighed and carefully wrapped in greaseproof paper. The cheese of choice at that time was Dunlop, a type of cheddar but paler in colour, taking its name from the Ayrshire town where it was manufactured. Butter was cut from a huge slab and knocked into neat rectangles with wooden butter pats. Many goods were sold in bulk in the grocer's shop - oatmeal, sugar, rice – and expertly packaged into brown paper bags. In this same row of red sandstone shops, I remember the Buttercup Dairy, at that time a well-known chain. But I remember it for the wrong reasons. As a small child I was dispatched one day to the shops to get some butter, and instead of going to the usual grocers, I wandered into the Buttercup and got the wrong kind. Mummy was not pleased and told me I was a stupid little girl. That put me off going into shops on my own until I was well into my teens! The green grocers and the chemist would have been visited no doubt but practically anything you wanted was delivered. The medicine cupboard of the 30s had no great array of pills and creams. In the bathroom it could supply Milk of Magnesia or Syrup of figs, TCP or boracic powder, Andrew's fruit salts, Gregory's powder and iodine for cuts and scratches, bandages, sticking plaster and lint and not much else. Toothpaste of course and on top lay my father's shaving brush and cut-throat razor well out of my reach. On a hook hung the leather strop which sharpened this frightening cutting instrument.

On the occasional shopping visit to Glasgow I was very excited, whether going by train or tram car. Mummy seemed to favour the big department stores of either Buchanan Street or Sauchiehall Street, where on every floor there was an enclosed cashier's desk. At the counter where purchases were made, the money and invoice would be put into a metal container and whizzed overhead on a wire cable to the cashier, and then it would whizz back to the counter with receipt and change. Job done! I was soon familiar with the names of these big stores – Pettigrew and Stephens, Coplands, Dalys, Rowans, MacDonalds, and Paisleys, the latter, well known as a stockist of school uniforms for the many schools of Glasgow and surrounding areas. The splendid Argyll Arcade was a good place to window shop on a cold wet day. For books, important items in the Hutchison household, there might be a visit to John Smith's and then to Cooper's, with its all-pervading smell of coffee, for extras. At Christmas time, with excitement in the air, there would be a visit to Santa Claus in his grotto in one of the big stores. But the scenes of the streets themselves were more interesting to me than the shops. The pavement artists, the flower girls, an occasional mounted policeman, the rattle of trams, the horses and carts by the pavement, the patient horses with their nosebags from which any spilled grain was a source of delight to the numerous house sparrows that were common in the streets.

At one spot the hurdy-gurdy man was usually to be found playing his barrel organ, his monkey, dressed in a red jacket a-top, and his cap lying on the pavement to receive the passers-by's pennies. And then there were the newsvendors crying, "Times, News, Citizen!" (emphasis on the last syllable). Alas now, I believe only one of these evening papers remains in circulation.

My very first friend was Jewish. We were about 3 or 4 years of age when we shyly made contact on the quiet road where we both lived. Soon we were daily playmates. Giffnock even then had a large Jewish population, an even bigger one as time went on. Many Jewish immigrants arrived in Glasgow in the 19th and early 20th centuries, as well as many Irish. The Jews settled in the Gorbals area and around Garnethill, where they established an early synagogue. As they became more prosperous, just as many native Glaswegians were doing, they sought a better life out in the southern suburbs of Giffnock and neighbouring areas such as Clarkston and Netherlee.

By the late 30s the Jewish population of Giffnock was large enough for it to have its own synagogue but with yet further expansion I believe a newer, larger one was built in the 60's.

Elaine's father was a businessman. She had an older sister, and a baby brother. Although in the early 30's with the rise of the Nazi party and its hatred of Jews and with many fleeing to safer environments, even in this country there was still some suspicion of them or even outright anti-Semitism, and sometimes in high places too. Hore-Belisha, who gave his name to the orange lollipop road crossings, was said to be an anti-Semitic. There was no such prejudice in my family and they appeared to be perfectly happy that I had a little Jewish friend.

My much older cousin Walter sometimes referred to them as the Jordan Highlanders, but he meant no harm. He was already a suave 30-something young man about-town, a buyer in lingerie. Walter was the one that introduced Andrew to some of Glasgow's nightlife I was later told.

On one or two occasions I was taken out by the Jewish family for a country picnic. The first time I was asked on my return if I had had a good time. The enthusiastic reply in the affirmative, I believe, was extended by my saying "but we got funny bread" – doubtless the unleavened variety. At one point there was an enforced break in our friendship when the older sister developed scarlet fever. This was scary news for in these days it was a serious illness and could even be fatal. Fortunately there was no further spread even within the family and the neighbourhood would have been mightily relieved. I had already had whooping cough and measles would come before schooldays.

And before school there was much to learn - nursery rhymes, playing with coloured pencils, being read stories. My favourite book was "Little Black Sambo", one that was much later deemed to be quite unsuitable for a child. And I had a golliwog that I called Sambo and loved dearly. Once on being told I had been naughty and nobody liked a naughty little girl I ran to fetch him from my bedroom and clutching him tightly I had announced, "Sambo likes me bad". At any rate neither the story nor Sambo himself ever prejudiced me as I grew up against black people. Indeed I later chose to have a black doll whom I called Vincent, and at that time Paul Robeson was enchanting people with his "Ole Man River".

I won't give up Sambo. Cutting from *The Bulletin*.

I was still quite small, when Mummy had to have some minor operation (I didn't, of course, understand anything of this) and I was taken south by my Aunt Winnie for a while. One day she took my cousin Ian, two years my senior, and me into Central London where, because I was jealous of Ian's Mickey Mouse, she bought me a Minnie Mouse in her red spotted skirt. We went to Buckingham Palace to see the Changing of the Guard, and also went to lunch at a hotel, where in the restaurant, there was a raised area where a small ensemble played light music while we ate. This was exciting grownup stuff.

A lift on cousin Barrie's car.

Before school I had copied the handwriting from incoming envelopes, especially varied as the Christmas cards popped through the letterbox. I also tried to copy the mathematical symbols on sheets of paper that Daddy had discarded. He hoped, I'm sure, for another mathematician in the family, a hope that, in my case, was later sadly dashed. For the moment I loved scribbling and drawing patterns on any paper I could find. My teacher mother taught me the alphabet and I could read and write just a little before going to school.

School was the local Primary near the station on the grandly named Academy Road. It had been built and opened in the year of George V's coronation (1911), as the village suburb of Giffnock gradually expanded. And the Orchardhill Parish Church, which we attended as a family, had also been opened at the beginning of the 20th century. Before that time some large mansion houses were built for wealthy businessmen and industrialists from Glasgow, who fancied life in the green acres to the south of the city. Once at school one of my playmates, appropriately named Rose, was daughter of the gardener at one of these large houses. Access to the gardener's stone cottage was not far from our road end.

I had been impatient to get to school but once there my enthusiasm for it soon wore off as it also did for Sunday school and my memories of it are few. The classroom backed onto the railway line. I loved the sound of the trains slowing down to reach the station and, better still, when they pulled out on their way to Busby and beyond. *Choo, choo, choo, choo* with the accompanying clouds of steam. I clearly remember the janitor arriving with a huge white enamel pitcher containing Horlicks which was distributed to the children at mid-morning break before the days of school milk or dinners. Huge posters on the wall depicted the seasons and we had lined jotters on which we learned to write simple words and phrases, and were introduced to the world of numbers. Our introduction to music was by means of a little percussion band with drums, triangles, tambourines. At least we learned something about rhythm. Sometimes we had dancing to music and I remember once playing "Ring o' Roses" in a big room and wetting my knickers, as I was too shy to ask to be excused in front of so many people. Things improved once out of the baby class, but I never really liked the tiled corridors and the smell of disinfectant and carbolic soap, and was always happy when it was time to go home.

Elderberries.

The road down to school was still partly rural, lined by some shrubs and flowery banks, and it passed an area of open ground where local kids played and the community bonfire night was held on November the 5th. A bridge crossed the tree-lined stream and soon I found myself at the main Kilmarnock Road as it was known then. No rush of traffic, just the occasional tram or car so it was safe and easy to cross. Now of course I had school friends, some of them living quite near. One day some of us were tempted to eat berries off a fruiting tree by our homeward path. On discovering this my mother was thrown into a panic, fearing I had eaten something deadly. As it turned out they were elderberries which certainly can't have been very appetising but were not poisonous. After all they are often used to make homemade wines. Occasionally on the way home I lingered at the bridge over the burn. One day a small boy beckoned me down to the bank. All he wanted to do was show me his willy, but I was totally unimpressed and turned for home. On another occasion, coming out of school, a bully-boy snatched my hat and wouldn't relinquish it. A tussle ensued. Being a bit older by this time, I eventually slipped my school bag off my shoulder and whacked him over the head with it. He dropped the hat and retreated to laughter from the onlookers. He never troubled me again.

The girls all had skipping ropes and there was a 30's craze for the yo-yo and toy guns that popped when the trigger was pulled. Pea-shooters were also great fun, especially when we tried to hit a neighbour's kitchen window. A family of boys who lived in one of the nearby big houses were sometimes watched through the keyhole of their green-painted garden side gate by a small girl. They played cowboys and Indians with wigwams on the lawn, and some of them sported Red Indian feathered headdress. This was altogether more exciting than girls play! Eventually I was allowed in to join them and I was thrilled.

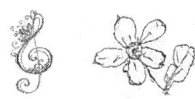

Two daily newspapers were delivered to our home – one the "Glasgow Herald" for serious adult reading, and "The Bulletin" which always had lots of pictures. As I grew up these were often my means of understanding something of the wider world. Here would be King George and Queen Mary on public engagements, the Queen always with her toque hat and choker of pearls, another day there might be pictures of the Yorks and the two princesses or the Prince of Wales in plus-fours or sometimes with raincoat and bowler hat on visits to factories and mines. There were pictures of Hitler and Mussolini, of Oswald Mosely and his black-shirts, of Mahatma Gandhi in sandals and a white shawl – to me a strange bespectacled little man. Pictures too of flying boats and the latest automobiles and locomotives, and well-known figures of stage and screen like Charlie Chaplin, George Formby, Gracie Fields or Noel Coward. On a lighter note the paper carried a daily comic strip of a certain Mr Peter Potter who blundered through every-day occurrences rather like a forerunner to Mr Bean. But there were also photographs of men in dole-queues and scenes of great poverty, especially in the big industrial towns where unemployment was so high it reached almost three million in the early 30s.

The decade has often been depicted in overwhelmingly negative terms and it is true that it was tough for many. But there was another side to it. With a gradual recovery from the deep Depression came a rise in consumerism. Electricity which was absent from the majority of homes in the twenties was now being used on a grand scale with many homes at last receiving it. This meant employment for more and led to the manufacture of many electrical gadgets – vacuum cleaners, wirelesses, irons, electric kettles, and other goods.

A relaxation of the wage cuts of the early 30s meant, for those in employment, a better quality of life. There was a boom in house building, as was evident in Giffnock, and more cinemas and dance halls were built. More cars were manufactured - the famous Baby Austin 7, the Ford 8, the Morris 8, and others. Petrol was cheap, around 1/- per gallon, and so the roads got busier. The Hutchisons acquired their first car, a Rover, in 1937.

Uncle George Wishart (my great uncle), had been bolder, having bought a big car back in the twenties. It was lovingly cared for over many years and he was still being driven around in it into his nineties, when he finally stopped driving himself.

I had not known home life without electricity, but my grandmother refused to have it installed and persevered with gas lighting, with its remarkably white light shining through the gas-mantles, until the end of her life. Our wireless had a funny yellow front with black knobs and if I peeped behind I could see its strange silvery valves. Later it was replaced by a more modern one in Bakelite. News bulletins were religiously followed by the others. For me there was "Children's Hour" around tea-time hosted by Auntie Kathleen. On Saturday evenings the wireless was tuned into a programme called "In Town Tonight" with Henry Hall's orchestra. The introductory music was part of the Knightsbridge section of Eric

Coates' London Suite. I loved it then and I like it still after all these long years. Hearing it, even now, it takes me straight back into the living room at Giffnock. The wireless allowed the popular songs of the time right into the family environment – "Ole Man River", "Tea for Two", "Smoke Gets in Your Eyes", "The Teddy Bears Picnic", "The Lambeth Walk," and George Gershwin's "Love Walked In". Entertainers became more than mere names – Harry Lauder, Gracie Fields, George Formby, Jack Buchanan and more. The 30s saw a great burgeoning of cinemas, Giffnock getting its own Art Deco "Tudor" around 1936 or so.

Many of the population, even in poor areas, flocked to the pictures or the "flicks" on a weekly basis or even oftener. My father frowned on such decadent entertainment and it wasn't till much later that he was finally persuaded to see one or two notable films. Mummy on the other hand in time became quite a fan, especially during the war years. I was taken – who wasn't? – to see "Snow White and the Seven Dwarfs"; released in 1937 and I was enchanted and the dwarfs' song "Heigh Ho, Heigh Ho, It's Off to Work We Go" was catchy. Shirley Temple was the child star of the screen in the States at the time and I was taken to see her too. I even named one of my new dolls Shirley, in her honour.

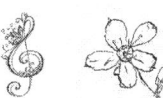

There were many momentous events taking place as I grew up which I was aware of through the wireless, the wonderful Bulletin newspaper, and by hearing my elders and their friends discussing issues of the day. The building of the magnificent Cunard luxury liner had been held up because of the Depression, but it was finally launched on Clydeside by the Queen in 1934. By the time of the "Queen Mary"'s maiden voyage, Andrew and David were busy at the dining room table fitting together the pieces of a large jigsaw of her and I became an awestruck spectator. Letters with special stamps to mark King George's Silver Jubilee dropped through the letterbox in 1935, the same year that the red telephone kiosks were introduced to become a feature of city streets and quiet corners in villages for decades to come. Sadly the King died in January of the following year and all the newspapers and the wireless reported this sad news. I was morbidly fascinated by the pictures of his lying-in-state at Westminster Hall, his four sons standing guard at the corners of the catafalque.

That same year, Mussolini invaded Abyssinia and Hitler, by now the German Chancellor, proudly hosted the Olympic Games in Berlin.

Pictures began to appear of the American divorcee, Wallis Simpson, in the company of the new King Edward. Some of these pictures were of them cruising together on a yacht, and the wireless often mentioned Fort Belvedere where they spent weekends together. It could have been on the moon for all I knew, but much later I discovered that it was in Windsor Great Park! By the end of the year came the Abdication crisis, the intricacies of which a child couldn't possibly understand. Nevertheless, on the evening of the 10th of December, exactly a week after my sixth birthday, my father took me on his knee to listen as the King announced to the nation that he was giving up the throne. This was history in the making and I remember that moment well. Now we had a new King and Queen, and 1936 subsequently became known as the year of the three kings.

In May 1937 came the Coronation and there were pictures of horse-drawn state carriages, crowds, flags, men in ornate uniforms, ladies in long dresses with tiaras and jewels. All school children were issued with celebratory mugs. Tea caddies and shortbread tins featured pictures of the new Royals, and the stirring Coronation March, "Crown Imperial", by William Walton, was first heard over the airwaves, but is loved to this day by many, including me.

The streamlined locomotive, 'the Coronation Scot', in its metallic blue and white striped livery, completed the London to Glasgow journey in six and half hours, reaching 114mph and thus breaking the existing speed record. It never subsequently enjoyed the fame of the 'Flying Scotsman' but it was a beautiful locomotive that excited my train-loving brothers who went into Glasgow to see it arrive.

In the late 30s I was aware that there was a civil war going on in Spain and can remember it being discussed between my brothers, and of course there was news of it on the wireless which I didn't really understand. In fact it was all totally confusing until much later the bare bones of the matter were explained to me. It was a tussle between the two political extremes, so threatening to world peace, Fascism and Communism. Franco – I knew his face well enough from pictures – was supported by Germany and Italy and received arms from them, while the Soviet communists did the same for the Republican side. Many idealistic young men from different countries joined what was known as the International Brigade to aid the Republicans, believing that communism was preferable to fascism, and many died in this cause. It was a bloody and destructive war but nothing to what would come a few years later.

Much nearer home, 1938 brought a peaceful international event to Glasgow, the Empire Exhibition. Glasgow had hosted two previous exhibitions in Kelvingrove Park in 1888 and in 1901. This one occupied a large site in Bellahouston Park on the south side of the city and was dominated by the much photographed three-hundred-foot modernistic tower designed by Thomas Tate. I was taken to the Exhibition on several occasions by my mother. She had bought me a new red blazer for the event, hoping she might be able to spot me in the crowd, if I strayed from her side. The Exhibition was opened in May but thereafter followed a wet summer, it was said, the wettest in south-west Scotland for close on a hundred years. I can't say I remember the rain but I do remember broad avenues, modern buildings, fountains and cascades, bands playing, and ice-cream and toffee apples freely available for treats. There were "Pavilions" for the different Dominions and Colonies of the Empire, highlighting their products such as New Zealand lamb and butter. "Palaces" for Industry and Art, a concert hall, and lots of other venues and exhibits. We visited the Clachan where tweeds, tartans and spinning wheels were displayed, and a Crazy House where everything was crooked and at odd angles, and where mirrors made me look funny. I loved it! The large Amusement park had a high switch-back railway which Andrew and David enjoyed on their frequent evening visits with season tickets. That was way too scary for me but I did enjoy a lot of it including riding a 'horse' on a Merry-go-round, and going on a dodgem car area with my adventurous 'up-for-it' mother. She had a go at a coconut shy too, but I don't think she won anything. There was all the fun of the Fair on offer, fortune tellers and all.

British Empire Exhibition

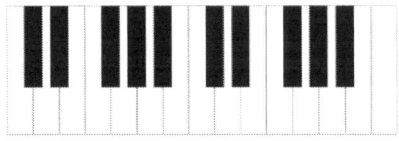

Each summer the Hutchison family decamped to the island of Arran for the summer vacation, always for July and sometimes for the long two months of school holidays. I recall nothing of my earliest visits but there are photographs of me there as a baby and a toddler. Gradually I absorbed the sights and sounds, even the smells, which became so dear to me.

The Hutchison love affair with this lovely island did not start with me nor with my parents. The Barrowman grandparents had holidayed here before the turn of the century. My mother, in some of her jottings, remembered a holiday at a thatched cottage at Bennan with her parents and older sister around 1890, when she was a small girl. The cottage belonged to the local blacksmith, James Currie. On his retiral he moved to Glenside at Kilmorie. The Barrowmans followed, where all seven of their children would have run wild and played in the very house and surroundings which became so special to me and my brothers before me.

Daddy had a previous connection with Arran too, having studied its geology for his second degree, and he often reminisced about holidaying with his widowed mother at the remote Craw, a tiny township perched high above the shore in the north west of the island. He roamed the hills and shore, and could tell me of the run-rig system of farming practiced along the flat land by the road, on the geological 25ft raised beach, characteristic of so much of the Clyde coastline.

Rosalind on Arran.

The Craw looked out over the Kilbrannan Sound and the long arm of Kintyre. Beyond, to the south west, lies Northern Ireland from whence Grandma came. Perhaps there may have been something in the south west wind here that took her back to her childhood there. I never knew that Grandma but Daddy said that I sometimes reminded him of her by my quiet nature.

Before the advent of foreign travel for the majority, the Firth of Clyde, between the wars and long before, was a popular escape destination for the citizens of Glasgow and neighbouring towns. Lots of steamers carried the masses to their holiday islands of Cumbrae, Bute, and Arran, and to many watering places on the coastline such as Dunoon, Hunters Quay, Innellan, Campbeltown, and others.

Grandma Hutchison & Uncle George.

Much has been written about the Clyde steamers and my father seemed to know quite a lot of their history.

During my childhood it was the 'Glen Sannox' that left Winton Pier at Ardrossan and carried us the twelve miles or so to Arran, and virtually into another world. The steamer would edge away out of the harbour near where the Irish ferry was berthed, out by the little Horse Island with its gleaming white flurry of nesting terns and head towards the skyline of high granite hills.

'Glen Sannox'.

The 'Glen Sannox', a turbine ship of the Caledonian Steam Packet Co., had two yellow funnels. She had replaced the first ship of that name, a paddle, in 1925. A 'Duchess of Argyll' also sailed this route up until 1932 and the smaller 'Marchioness of Graham' with one funnel did likewise as late as 1958, when she was sold to Greece as a pleasure boat sailing the Aegean waters. There was also a 'Duchess of Montrose' and a 'Duchess of Hamilton', names reflecting the history of Arran's aristocratic landowners.

'Duchess of Montrose'.

'Duchess of Montrose' and 'Marchioness of Graham' at Whiting Bay Pier.

At the outbreak of war 'The Talisman' and other Clyde steamers were taken for minesweeping duties and the handsome paddle 'Jupiter', built only in early 1937, soon went to the Thames to serve as an anti-aircraft ship.

The 'Glen Sannox' was a turbine ship and the engine room could easily be viewed by passengers. Daddy being interested in the dynamics of the engine always took us to see it too. The two engineers were almost within touching distance as they stood before a range of shining dials and clocks on which ½ Speed, Full Speed Ahead, and more were displayed. With ringing bells and sparkling busy pistons we were on our way.

A broad staircase mid-ship took us down to the restaurant. Here proper meals were served at tables laid with starched white tablecloths and napkins, and shiny cutlery and glasses which tinkled with the throb of the engines. A raised ridge around the table edges was designed to prevent plates and glasses sliding off, if the sea was rough. In these early days a waitress, properly dressed in black dress and white lacy apron and cap, would serve the passengers. All so very civilised in contrast to the modern rabble of a self-service café with sausage rolls and packaged sandwiches, portions of chips, tea and coffee served in polystyrene beakers.

Sometimes in the steerage area of the ship there might be a couple of calves sewn into sacks or a little gathering of sheep in a small pen, bleating now and then, as they stood in a scattering of their droppings. Occasionally there might be a container with tiny fluffy day-old chicks; all of interest to a child. On very rare occasions there could be a car on deck. Before the advent of roll-on-roll-off ferries in the 60s, cars had to be driven up to the deck on two planks, a tricky business, and one which my brother Andrew accomplished after the black Rover had been purchased in the late 30s.

First port of call was into the magnificent Brodick Bay with its backdrop of wooded slopes, sheltering the red sandstone castle, and rising above, the peak of Goatfell. The sandy beach was lined with brightly coloured bathing huts. The pier was usually crowded with holiday makers and with much shouting between deck and pier as friends recognised each other. After careful manoeuvring and the throwing of ropes the gangway was positioned and a stream of holidaymakers disembarked. Now the ship sailed on around the headland to the sheltered waters of Lamlash Bay with the protecting Holy Isle half a mile off shore. Our final destination was round passed the lighthouse on Holy Isle and the next headland, and into Whiting Bay pier. Because the waters here are shallow the pier was long, and on a wet or windy day, very long. I believe it was the longest pier on the Firth of Clyde. After the long walk a wooden booth had to be passed, where pier dues of 2d were demanded. My father usually grumbled at this.

Brodick Bay, Arran.

Fortunately it was only hand luggage that had to be carried along that long pier, for a few days before our departure, two large cabin trunks would have been picked up from home, all expertly packed by Mummy, with sheets, towels, clothes, bathing things, fishing gear, and much else. They would be awaiting us now at Glenside.

Now for the bus which would take us on the last part of our journey. Arran in these days had several small, independent bus companies – Lennox, Ribbeck, Bannatyne, and Gordon. Ours was Stewart's, based in a very modest garage at Corriecravie. While on holiday we sometimes saw these various buses on the roads on their "Round-the-Island" trips, or their so-called "Mystery tours". Alas, there wasn't much mystery, for apart from the road around the island there were only two others that crossed the island, the String in the north, and the Ross in the south. Possible variations were severely limited and mystery scarce.

Wild garlic.

Soon our bus would be rumbling along the road above the shore, uphill and southwards on its torturous route by Largybeg and down into the steep wooded gully at Dippen, where the road was often wet and smelt of wild garlic. There were other difficult bends in the road as it crossed wooded burnsides, and on these steep bends the bus almost came to a halt as the driver warred with his gear changes, for then and long after, gear changes involved double de-clutching. There were stops at road ends, where people waited to greet friends or receive parcels off the bus, the men in thick trousers, if a good day with rolled up sleeves, watch-chains hanging from waistcoat pockets, and cloth caps on their heads. In fine weather the women were mostly dressed in floral pinafores, hair usually in a bun, and always, it seemed, with one or two border collies at their heels.

Pladda & Ailsa Craig.

Once passed the road-end to Kildonan below us and the offshore island of Pladda and its lighthouse, the view opened out over the Bennan farmland of small fields where brown and white Ayrshire cows grazed. Alisa Craig, the volcanic plug affectionately known as Paddy's Milestone, we could now see lying out in the water like an upturned pudding basin. The finest curling stones in the world have long been quarried here, and it is also home to a large colony of gannets. Passed Shannochie and up the last hill to our destination, known locally as Butterhill, although it doesn't appear on any map that I know of and I can only guess at the origin of the name. At the start of the holiday this was a wonderful spot, the beginning proper of the annual adventure, but when over, it was a sad place as we waited for the bus that I wished would never come, the telegraph wires humming a little, a soft air gentle on my face, and harebells nodding on the bank where the bus would stop.

But on arrival now, it was all excitement as we walked along the rough farm road between beech and hawthorn hedges and a lush growth of grasses and wild flowers, including the frothy sweet smelling Meadowsweet, or as Mummy called it "Queen of the Meadow", one of the very first wild flowers I could name.

Meadowsweet.

Round the last right-angled bend and we were soon at Glenside, where Mrs. Currie was there to welcome us.

Glenside Farmhouse.

The welcome, always warm, was extended into the farm kitchen where fresh milk, a bowl of new-laid eggs, butter, and a selection of freshly baked scones would be ready "to start us off" as she used to say. The large black kettle would be near the boil on the kitchen range.

After refreshments we all had our priorities. Mummy had the unpacking to do and beds to make up, Daddy had to check over his fishing gear, his books, and supply of tobacco. My brothers were soon off somewhere, and I had to visit all the farm animals – the dogs and cats, kittens if there were any, my favourite pigs, and the two Clydesdale horses in the stable if they were not out working in the fields.

During the 30s several vans would come to the yard on different days, bringing all the food essentials and more – soap, candles, paraffin, sweets, tobacco. Kirby grips and elastic, and long sticky yellow fly papers to hang up in the kitchen to trap the flies and bluebottles that always gathered where food was present. There were fewer vans by the time war came, and

then one of our first walks would be the half-mile or so across the moorland path to Shannochie and to the small thatched, white-washed post
office with its red letter box on the wall. It was run by the friendly and efficient Jenny Hamilton who always greeted my parents as old friends. It was
a tiny place but quite an Aladdin's Cave and if not quite providing goods
from the proverbial needle to an anchor, it came close.

Shannochie PO.

With two shopping bags full we would return homewards across the
moorland path between clumps of heather not yet in flower in July and
small grassy patches dotted with the bright yellow, four-petalled flowers of
tormentil, and the small white or pale lilac heads of eyebright. At the end
of the path, close to a fresh water spring, we always looked for the lovely
butterwort.

Tormentil.

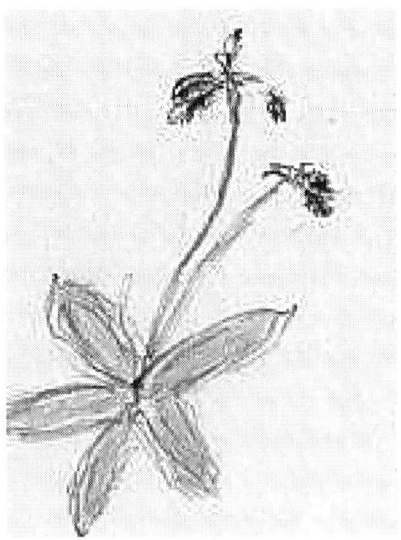

Butterwort.

Depending on the weather conditions in June, its blue violet-like flowers might be over but the fleshy yellow-green leaves were always there, leaves that I learnt from an early age were able to catch and digest tiny flies. It was on Arran that I first aspired to become a botanist and Mummy was my tutor, for she had loved wild flowers long before me. I still have a gift she received from my father before they were married. It is a copy of the Rev. C.A. John's "Flowers of the Field". The inscription on the fly-leaf is dated 31st May 1911.

The kitchen of the farmhouse was where we spent most of our time when not outdoors. It had a lovely pale wooden dresser adorned with an array of plates, cups, bowls, and differently shaped and coloured jugs, another long side-dresser, kitchen table, a curtained bed handy for hiding things in, and the black kitchen range which had to be kept going no matter whether the weather was cool or hot for the cooking was done upon it. Daddy always brought a small Primus paraffin camping stove as an addition. He seemed to take charge of this, as he did of the lamps, filling up the paraffin and trimming the wicks. Apart from candles they were the only means of lighting.

The house had no running water either and the white enamel pails which stood on the scullery floor had to be replenished from the yard pump. I didn't master the functioning of this until I was a good deal older. Then it was a most satisfying experience to see the fresh water flush into the pail as a result of rhythmic up and down movements of the handle. Dishes were washed in an enamel basin with water heated in the kettle and some of our own daily ablutions were often carried out here in another basin. The lack of a bath mattered little as we bathed in the sea most days, but I do have faint memories of being bathed in a tin bath in front of the fire when I was little. It still hung from a hook on the scullery wall.

The privy was some distance from the back door, down the length of an adjoining cottage and the barn. It was a small lean-to with a corrugated iron roof. The door was secured by a simple 'sneck' and one had to sit on a varnished wooden shelf with its necessary hole. Underneath, discreetly hidden by a wooden door, was the pail that was emptied for us daily. The thin Izal toilet rolls of the day were supplemented by strips of newspaper hung on a hook. This D.C. was not, I suspect, sited for our convenience (an unfortunate choice of words) but for its relative proximity to the large midden. Here the sweepings from the byre, stable, pig sty, and henhouse would all be added. When broken down this was carted to the fields and ploughed into the sandy soil.

In the early 30s, with the Depression past its worst, the small farmers and crofters on Arran were gradually recovering from extreme hardship, but nevertheless the long-established habit of moving out of their winter quarters to let them during the summer months to holidaymakers doubtless made a small but welcome addition to their income. The Curries let their farmhouse and sometimes the 'wee house' as well and moved into the barn for the summer months. Here they had two beds for themselves and their two sons. The cooking was done on a black kitchen range, the solid wooden kist, used for storing oatmeal and flour served as a seat for two at the wooden table. Other wooden kitchen chairs were the most comfortable they had. Close to the window, which looked out over the stackyard was a small mirror where Dan would have shaved, and by the window's edge a string of rosettes were displayed, proof that not a few 1st and 2nd class prizes had been won at local shows over recent years, for Dan, as they said 'had an eye for a good beast'. In the barn was another dresser decked with plates and crockery of different types and patterns.

One thing I never understood was the big corn-mill here. When in use it would have been powered by horses walking round and round the circular treadmill which lay outside the back of the barn. The barn was kept spotless, with near daily scrubbings, finished off with fancy patterned edges applied with pipe clay. Even the doorstep was given a frilly white-patterned edge.

As a young child mornings were happily spent around the farm with the animals. There were eggs to collect from the old, open rickety henhouse - dangerously open but thankfully there were no foxes on the island. I helped to feed fluffy little chicks from a bowl in which oatmeal had been soaked. Tiny potatoes, too small for the table, were washed in a pail of water, then boiled for the hens and the pigs. I watched the horses in their stalls being prepared for the day's work and I always spent time with the pigs which I simply adored. Whenever missing, they always looked for me at the pig sty!

Meanwhile my brothers were more than likely on the little 9-hole golf course or down at Lagg to meet up with other young folk who, like us, returned year after year to the same cottages and farmhouses in the district, one family even returning each summer all the way from London. At the golf course a large green-painted wooden shed served as the clubhouse where golf items, postcards, sweets, and soft drinks could be bought. When my cousins Barrie and Ian came from Leicester to holiday at Lagg hotel, Uncle Willie indulged us here with toffees and lemonade.

Weather permitting, the afternoons were spent on the lovely sandy beach, quite a distance for little legs, but the effort was well worthwhile. The numerous families who came here all had their recognised patches where they picnicked and undressed among the marram grass for their swim in the sea.

In my earliest years paddling was enough for me. When the tide was out I had to walk over the sand, avoiding patches of small pebbles that hurt my bare feet and over the wave patterns left by the outgoing tide and wriggly worm casts, before my toes would reach the water. Now I could wiggle my feet in the sand to disturb little crabs, being careful to avoid the occasional jellyfish that I was warned could sting. Over the sparkling water lay Alisa Craig. Sometimes gannets from there made their spectacular dives, while a few gulls and the pied oyster catcher would call from a nearby long dyke of rock. These long fingers are characteristic of the island, lines of igneous rock intruding into the softer red sandstone, the basic geological bedrock of the south of the island. Not that I knew that then.

2½ year old Rosalind, paddling in 1933.

After a little picnic there might be ball games, and the serious building of sandcastles. My sandcastles were modest, just pies really, but Andrew in particular was a master builder and produced elaborate edifices, sometimes with moats around and decorated with seaweed flags for my delight – or perhaps for his own!

All too soon it was time to make for home, crossing the short turf where green grasshoppers chirruped and tiny blue butterflies flew among the flowers, to join the cart track which wound up the cliff. Andrew and David nearly always showed off by climbing straight up a very steep slope over clumps of bird's foot trefoil and bloody cranesbill, to wait for us at the top. Up the length of a field took us passed the cottages at Lenamhor where open doors revealed linoleum floored lobbies with perhaps a bicycle leaning against the wall. Out at the back, towels and bathing things would be

40

out to dry, ready for the next day. The last part of the walk home was often accomplished on my father's shoulder. I was tired but happy.

Bird's foot trefoil.

If back in time I loved to go to the byre and watch the evening milking. There were four cows, three of them milkers at a time I think, rejoicing, in floral names – Buttercup, Daisy, Clover, and Violet. Mrs Currie sat on her wooden stool, head against the cow's flank while her deft fingers coaxed the frothy milk into the pail, held firmly between her knees. The initial pinging sound of the milk hitting the bottom of the pail soon changed to a soft purring sound. Other holidaymakers came with their little milk cans each evening for supplies. Some of the milk was for us, some was saved for making butter, and there was usually a calf or two who fed noisily with slurping sounds from a pail. There was no such thing as pasteurising milk on these small farms, so it was literally straight from cow to jug. The cows, lovely horned creatures stood patiently in their stalls as all this was going on, with perhaps a flick of an ear, a swish of tail, and occasionally the more spectacular arrival of a cowpat into the stone channels of the byre. Then Buttercup and her pals would be turned out to pasture again till morning milking.

Within a day or two of our arrival at Glenside a panama-hatted gentleman would ride into the yard on his white pony. This was the Rev. Norman Wright, bringing to Mummy what David had once described as his 'peas offering'. For a good number of years Mummy had been inveigled into playing the harmonium in the parish church during her stay on holiday. In her youth she had learned to play the American organ at home, with her father's encouragement, so she made the best she could of this old instrument in the church for several Sundays. Mr Wright's visit was to formalise the arrangement for another year. He didn't just bring peas but other produce, perhaps even strawberries from his large garden. He also kept bees and a couple of pigs, and the ground of the glebe gave pasture for his pony.

So, holiday or not, on Sundays we were marched down the rough cart track to the 18th century church sitting above the Kilmorie water. This same burn runs down through the woods to the hamlet of Lagg, with its well-known hostelry. The small hotel has a wonderful site with colourful gardens and a lawn bordering the burn, where visitors often enjoyed afternoon tea. It sported a couple of palm trees (Cordyline), plants which can be found in several spots round the island, blessed as it is with the warming effect of the Gulf Stream. The one big drawback to Lagg was the midge population, which on damp evenings especially, could spoil this idyllic spot, the air redolent of midge repellant. Lagg means a hollow, and that is just what it is, down by the burnside and surrounded on all sides by woodland. From here the path to the shore is known locally as Lovers Walk.

Cordyline.

Lagg Hotel.

It was along this path to the burn, between Lagg and the sea where Daddy taught me to fish, with a proper rod and reel and fly. I don't think we ever caught a lot, just an occasional trout, but I did learn how to reel it in, till Daddy retrieved it in a net. Once an eel took my bait, but the long wriggly body was too snake-like for me so I dropped the rod and retreated to a safe distance.

My father fished this stretch of water of a summer evening with Mr McLaren, a Glasgow teacher like himself. Mr McLaren was not only a keen angler but was quite obsessed with the hobby of fly tying. He had a large collection in neat boxes and some specimens on the lapels of his jacket and even on his hat. He and Daddy fished for brown trout from the deep brown pools, always hoping for a silver sea trout. Either was delicious fried in oatmeal.

They were concerned one year to find nets had been placed at the mouth of the burn to catch sea trout. This was of course an illegal practice.

Kilmorie Water in dry weather.

A highlight of the holiday was haymaking, when burn and beach took second place in my sights. The horses, gentle Clydesdales with huge feet and hairy fetlocks would be prepared in the stable with large collars and other paraphernalia, ready to pull the cutter. But first the edges of the hay field had to be scythed to allow horse and cutter room to manoeuvre. In my childhood every true countryman could use the scythe. It was a skilled job, swinging it in steady gentle rhythm to fell the upstanding grass in wide sweeps. To keep the blade really sharp there were often pauses to rub the edge on a stone or carborundum. The scythe came into use at other times of course, making paths or clearing ditches or hedge banks. The horse and cutter soon cut long rows of grass and clover and wild flowers. This was when even the children could be of use, turning the hay with forks and fluffing it up to get as much air and sun in as possible, a process called tedding.

Mummy with the Clydesdales.

Afterwards the lines were gathered up with large wooden rakes into small heaps or cocks. Children from around felt very important doing this, the boys always in short trousers, the girls in cotton summer frocks, for most made by their mothers. It now seems strange to look back on the tradition of summer frocks, coming out at the beginning of May and being worn during the three or four months of summer, regardless of the weather!

Haymaking might stretch over several days depending on the weather but I have memories of warm days when it was quite hot work. In deference to hot weather in these days, men working in the field would shed their jackets but, never that I could see, either their waistcoats or thick flannel shirts. How they must have roasted! At break times, freshly baked scones were brought out from the kitchen and as well as tea or milk there was a cooling drink – water in which oatmeal had been soaked. The collie dogs who had been lying in the shade of the hedge would come out for a bowl of water. After the small cocks of hay had weathered a little, they were broken up again and fluffed out and turned, eventually, to be built into ricks or haystacks, a skilled task done by two men, one below, one above. The rick was rounded off and eventually covered with tarpaulin and weighed down with ropes and bricks or stones, against rain and wind. Some of the hay was transported directly by horse and cart to the back of the byre or to the attic above the stable. The rest, in ricks, stood out in all weathers in the stackyard until required.

Occasionally the horse and cart came out for other reasons, to transport potatoes and carrots, or other things. A ride in the cart was always a holiday highlight.

After a busy day out of doors I would sleep like a top in my small bedroom with its skylight and box bed (and very hard mattress!). The upstairs bedrooms at Glenside were wood-lined. The boys slept in a room with two curtained box beds, my parents in a double bed with fancy iron bed-ends and brass knobs. All bedrooms at that time had washstands, with basins and ewers and china soap dishes, and of course the necessary chamber pots, items that nowadays are sold in antique shops as plant containers.

Most of my holiday here as a child was spent on the farm, at the beach, or by the burn but occasionally there were visits to the smiddy to watch the blacksmith busy at his anvil shoeing a horse or mending tools, or we went by bus to visit my uncle Tom holidaying at Brodick where he would take my cousin Douglas and myself out in a rowing boat and then buy us ice cream at the café. We also visited Glasgow friends, who rented a house at Strathwhillan from where there were wonderful views over the bay to the magnificent Arran hills, and the skyline known to all as the Sleeping Warrior. Just prior to the war when my brothers brought the car over there were excursions to Whiting Bay and over to the western coastline of the island, to Blackwaterfoot and Machrie.

The Old Rover at Glenside.

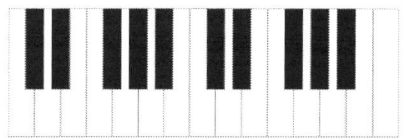

By the late 30s my brothers had become young men, having left school at Hutcheson's Boys Grammar School to embark on their chosen careers of Actuarial Science and Accountancy. This school had served them well, both academically and in the field of sport, and they had been proud to attend the same school as their father had many years before them. The school was founded back in 1641 by two successful Glasgow businessmen, George and Thomas Hutcheson. It early earned a reputation for high academic attainments, maintained well into the 20th century. John Buchan, the well-known Scottish writer was a pupil here and his brother Willie followed him, and was a contemporary of my father, in the same class, both born in the same year.

The school had an outstanding Classics master, James Cadell, who inspired in Father a life-long love of the Classics, in which he revelled as well as in the world of mathematics. But it was only because he had won, on merit, a bursary that he was able to attend this school at all. In his day the pupils were a mix of boys from the prosperous middle classes and of poor boys on a bursary. His brother George also won a bursary, which enabled him to go to a good school, this time Allan Glen's, but my Uncle Tom had to study at evening classes, while working, before qualifying as a pharmacist.

So by this time, in the late 30s, three men departed for the city in the mornings and one small girl walked her way to school. The boys, as they were still known, were there at mealtimes sitting opposite me. Although in the evenings they pursued their own interests, with their own friends, they often played bagatelle with me, or helped with jigsaws. At Christmas time it was they who decorated the tree on Christmas Eve and which I was not allowed to see until the big morning.

Christmas Day was either spent at home or at Grandma's. Here, my Aunt Dora, a domestic science teacher in London, home for a busman's holiday, did all the cooking. I remember I didn't like her stuffing nearly as much as the one Mummy made, but the Christmas pudding always contained carefully wrapped trinkets and 3d-bits. In the 30s and beyond, into the wartime years, Christmas decorations were largely made of brightly coloured paper, very cleverly cut so that they could be pulled apart as long lines, to be hung across the room. Everybody had them and in halls and classrooms they were often overdone, criss-crossing to the point of vulgarity. Folded paper balls and bells were common too, easily opened out like opening a book. It was usual to decorate picture rails with holly and for most there would be mistletoe hanging somewhere to surprise the unwary. The decorations for the tree and the lights, the tinsel, the bells and baubles were all carefully stored in a big box in the attic for the next year!

Often at weekends there would be visitors, and after the usual high tea, I would be packed off to bed while the adults talked and enjoyed some music. Mummy was a good singer and in her youth had received some professional training. I often heard her performing such things as Handel's "Where Ere You Walk", Mendelsohns's "On Wings' of Song", or Schubert's "Who is Sylvia" and his beautiful "To Music". These particular songs are marked in her well-used copy of Boosy + Co's Golden Treasury of Song, still among my collection of sheet music. Another of her songs was the sad little one from the Mikado – Willow Tit Willow. The practice of singing ballads at the piano on a Saturday or Sunday evening was something that Mummy was very familiar with as it was an Edwardian tradition. Her father had encouraged all his family to embrace the Arts, either art itself or music and literature. Two of my aunts trained at the Glasgow School of Art, one became a music teacher, and all could play the piano and sing tolerably well.

By next morning the smell of coffee and cigars would linger on the air. I loved fingering the cigar box itself and adored the smell.

Visiting and sharing meals among friends was the core of social life in the 30s. Most of my parent's friends were from the teaching and medical professions but some had been "out East" as it was described then. They had much posher houses than we had with fine rugs and ornaments brought back from India and elsewhere.

Sometimes I wandered into Mummy's bedroom and fingered the things lying on her dressing table – the silver-backed hand mirror, her powder puff, naughty little pot of rouge, and a bottle of "Evening in Paris" and thought it would be nice to be grown up. Occasionally my parents went to evening functions – I never knew where and I would be left in my brothers' care. They would come to kiss me goodnight before departing, Mummy in her long gown, Daddy in his dinner jacket and black tie, or more rarely in white tie and tails.

Another house visited in Giffnock was the home of the widow and family of one of Daddy's closest friends. Old granny lived with them. No doubt she was a nice old lady but I was a little scared of her; she was very, very deaf and had an old-fashioned ear trumpet that one had to speak into.

MANSEWOOD

A regular feature of my childhood was the weekend visit to my grand-mother. She lived with two unmarried daughters in a grey stone villa in Mansewood, an area not far from Giffnock. It was a household where edu-cation was much valued and there was often plenty talk about politics and world affairs. Books or papers were in evidence and I remember, as I grew up, seeing copies of Blackwoods Magazine, Chambers Journal, and of Punch lying upon a side table. These Journals were bought by my Aunt Jeannie, who soaked up the written word as blotting paper does ink. She had a heart condition and after qualifying with the Royal Academy of Mu-sic, had decided to stay at home to be a private piano teacher, working at her own pace, and allowing time for rest and the indulgence of her other two passions, of literature and gardening. Occasionally she would delight us with her playing of some of Mendelssohn's "Songs Without Words" or music by Percy Grainger.

It was here, with Grandma sitting in her cane-backed rocking chair, that the names of politicians and other figures of the time were bandied about – Lloyd George, Stanley Baldwin, General Smuts, Oswald Mosely, Hailie Selassi, Chang Kai Shek, Bertram Russell, Sir John Boyd Orr, and De Val-era, the anti-British Irish P.M. Only as I grew older did the significance of such people begin to make any sense to me.

Playing 'Happy Families' or 'The Minister's Cat' was more to my lik-ing and the latter certainly helped me to learn new words. The summer months allowed us to go into the garden, which was very different to ours and of course much longer established. Outside the back door there was a cobbled area where we often had tea and where a beautiful scented white lilac was prominent in early summer. Steps led up to the main walled gar-den where apples were trained on the back wall. A lawn had been specifically laid out to allow for bowling, a hobby of my late grandfather's, and round it were beds of roses and herbaceous plants for cutting for house decoration. Grandma loved to have lots of flowers in the house, particularly roses. In one corner, beside the summer house, a patch of alpine strawberries fruited well and in season I was allowed to pick them.

Roses painted by Aunt Chris.

In fine weather the brightly coloured deck chairs came out and the adults pursued their discussions in the sun. Sometimes an old croquet mallet and balls were produced, for that had been another of Grandpa's pastimes.

My grandfather, David Barrowman, had come from the country village of Saline in Fife from a family of blacksmiths and makers of ploughs. He came to Glasgow, I presume to better himself, and finally became Inspector of Poor and the Registrar for the Parish Council of Eastwood. He was anxious that his family should be educated in the widest sense for the days of the late 19th century. He had been widely read and was an admirer of Sir

Walter Scott, an admiration that I eventually shared, once into my early teens, and much to my grandmother's delight. He was also a keen gardener, a love that he passed on to all his daughters. His only son, Robert, had chosen agriculture as a career but sadly his studies were halted when he joined up as a Private in the Royal Fusiliers, studies that were never resumed, as he was among the hordes of young men killed in the Great War.

Barrowman grandparents.

I suspect, but do not have proof, that Grandpa's job as Inspector of Poor is what would first lead to his association with Arran, for it was a custom at the time for orphan children or those rescued from abject poverty or unsuitable families to be "boarded out" to countryside homes, and even in my time there were two such cases that I knew of, at Lagg and at Shannochie.

Grandpa Barrowman.

Every visit to Grandma ended by her going into a hall cupboard where she kept a selection of sweets and toffees. With a few of these and a 6d piece put into my pocket, it was time to go home and drop my sixpence into my piggy bank.

Kinnedar, Grandmother's house.

With Grandma, Mummy, Barrie & Ian in the Mansewood garden.

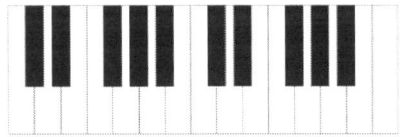

INTO THE HIGHLANDS

With the family's acquisition of a car my horizons widened somewhat. We visited Ayr and the birthplace of Robert Burns. Nearby Prestwick had already been on my radar with visits to old friends of my paternal grandmother from Northern Ireland. Prestwick to me meant walks along the Prom and ice-cream cones.

We visited Moffat when Grandma and the aunts were holidaying there and I was shown the Devil's Beef Tub, and told how the reivers had concealed the stolen cattle in this huge hollow. My imagination took wings at this.

It would have been 1937, I think, when we drove the long route up into the Highlands for a holiday at Gairloch. This was wild rugged country, so different to the gentle scenery of the south of Arran. Gairloch and its surroundings were of moorland and mountain, scattered houses, peat stacks, seaward views, and spectacular skyscapes and sunsets.

We lodged in a guesthouse where Gaelic was spoken. Mummy had to drag me away more than once from the kitchen door, where I was listening to the strange tongue. They must have been strict Sabbatarians in this household, for, on acknowledging our booking, they had stipulated that they didn't mind if we arrived late on Saturday evening but not after midnight! As if that was likely with a small child one of the party!

My memories of that holiday are patchy. I've no doubt there would have been some travelling around the district, certainly to

Loch Maree. By this time Daddy had been badly bitten by the angling bug and this was fine country for it. There must have been a golf course somewhere, I think, to satisfy Andrew and David. I do remember the weather was mixed, and I spent some wet hours down on the shore in front of the guest house, in wellies and sou'wester, with the little boy of the household. Till then, shores to me had meant sand and sandcastles. Here it was rocky and covered in seaweeds, some that made lovely popping noises when we deflated their bladders with our fingernails, and some with long brown straps that had been tossed ashore by stormy high-tides. And the rock pools were an eye-opener. My companion knew a lot more than I did and we happily poked around, finding tiny fish and crabs, purple sea anemones, and delicate red and pink seaweeds.

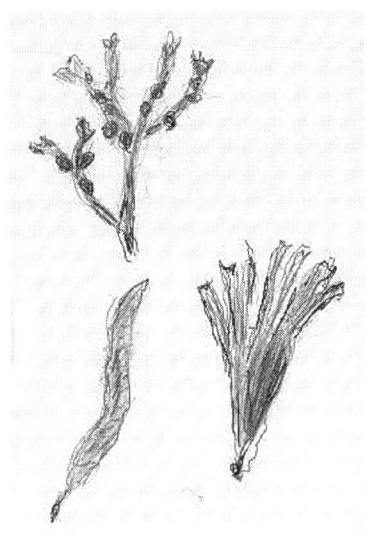

Brown seaweeds.

The holiday in the north-west was extended by going a little further north for a few days to Aultbea Hotel. This was my introduction to hotel life where huge breakfasts were on offer – porridge, kippers, bacon and eggs, cold hams and other meats, and an even bigger evening meal of several courses. I was allowed to stay up and partake of some of this largesse. Most, if not all, of the guests were here for the fishing and there seemed to be much talk about the day's catches.

The hinterland of this area is dotted with small lochs and streams, ideal for trout fishing, and the sea on the doorstep, so to speak. It was at Aultbea that I first encountered the custom of early morning tea being brought to the bedrooms by a maid and of shoes being put outside in the corridor at night, and they were there in the morning, shining like new.

Aultbea.

Before the advent of the car, there had been another short holiday to Skye, but what took us there I have no idea. I was quite small but remember a few things. For one, the taxi ride into Glasgow at an unearthly hour of the morning, with the streets near deserted, to catch the train up the west coast to board the ferry to Skye. I was told later that it had been a rough crossing, which had not worried me. We stayed at Portree in a house on the street and I didn't like the fact that the sand here was 'dirty', my description I was told, so unlike the lovely sand I was used to at Kilmorie. My second memory is of being taken to the local Free Church for morning service, possibly because my father would have been curious to see how things were done there. It was strange and the congregation stood for prayers and sat for psalms, which even to my young ear seemed so terribly unmusical.

During that holiday my brothers did some hill walking and, perhaps out of boredom, spent time at the harbour. Andrew became friendly with some of the fishermen here and one crew agreed to take him across the Minch, I presume to Stornoway, for a night or so. I clearly remember standing at the harbour, watching the boat disappear away up the Sound of Raasay. I had to be reassured that he would be back soon. David stayed on terra firma with the rest of us.

And there had been a brief stay in a caravan at St Andrews which was quite fun but I didn't take too kindly to the bracing wind off the North Sea.

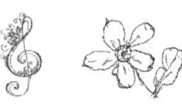

By Easter 1938, I was introduced to yet another type of country-side and way of life, one that was to become a hugely important part of the rest of my childhood and well beyond my youth. Some colleague or fishing companion of Daddy's had told him of the wonderful trout fishing to be enjoyed on Loch Awe, especially in spring.

So, that Easter we set off on, to me, the long car journey into the highlands of Argyllshire. I remember stopping for petrol at a quiet Shell pump and being saluted by AA men on their motorcycles with side-cars, where I have no doubt their tools and equipment would be carried. If your car carried an AA badge on the bonnet you were always saluted. Our destination was a lonely sheep-farm on the southern shore of the loch.

The boys spent a week or so fishing with their father, while Mummy and I walked along the lovely lochside road among wood-land, where the damp roadside banks were thick with primroses, patches of golden saxifrage, and a lush growth of mosses and ferns. I was introduced to the family and the farm and its animals. The youngest member of the family was Duncan, almost exactly the same age as myself, and we were soon good friends.

Primrose.

Mrs Crawford produced an array of interesting meals in spite of being nowhere near a shop. She kept a fine table with lovely silverware, cutlery and starched napkins, and meals served on pristine white tablecloths. Meals were cooked on a Rayburn in the kitchen, but to make life simpler she often prepared cold desserts in the mornings. It was here that I learned to prefer my semolina pudding cold and developed a liking for curds served with sugar, oatmeal, and rich cream! If the anglers were at all successful there would have been trout served baked or fried in oatmeal. One day they caught a pike, a large predatory fish and the enemy of trout. I have no doubt it was cooked and eaten, although it is a fish much despised. I have read that the French did at one time, maybe still do, make 'quenelles' with its meaty flesh.

Two features of the farmhouse were particularly pleasing in the comfortable sitting room – the huge log fires which were so delightful to sit around, and the Tilley lamps. There was no electricity in the house at that time but these gave a fine light, compared to the usual paraffin lamps. This delighted my father who could now relax with his books and Mummy with her crosswords, without too much eye-strain. The boys played board games with me such as Ludo, and Snakes and Ladders until my bedtime. The house was so comfortable, the family so friendly and welcoming, it was inevitable that we would be back and indeed we were frequently and over many years. The war however meant that my brothers would not accompany us for much longer.

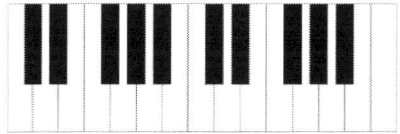

GLASGOW

During my growing years my father had been Head of the Mathematics Dept. at the Glasgow High School for Boys, a post I believe he loved. Before his war service he had left the teaching profession to become a lecturer in the Provincial Training College for Teachers, but eventually his love for teaching pupils rather than students, took him back to the classroom. When he was at the Boys' High, for some reason, I remember being taken, as a very small girl, to a Prize Giving Day there and watching the boys in their brown blazers mounting the platform to receive their prizes and thinking how very grown up they all looked. I was also taken to one of their Sports Days at Anniesland on the West side of the city. That was an occasion chiefly remembered for strawberry tarts and ice-cream!

Unknown to me, Mummy, always proud of her husband's abilities, had been pushing him to apply for a headmastership. At last that was secured for Hyndland School, one of Glasgow's largest at that time. One day I was told that we would be leaving Giffnock. I was quite broken-hearted, so much so that my mother found in my bedroom a little 'essay' that I had written, bemoaning this awful news and recording all the things I would miss – the house, the garden, the woodland, and all my little friends.

The plan had been to find a house in the west end of the city where my father would be closer to his work. Not having been successful in finding something suitable, they decided, as a temporary solution, to rent a flat in Hyndland itself. The threat of, and eventu-

al outbreak of war put an end to that plan and the 3rd floor flat was
to become home for the rest of my childhood and youth.

Father in the 30s.

At last, towards the end of 1938 the day arrived when I was parked out with friends, and therefore did not witness the actual removal. I was taken a few hours later straight to our new home by my brothers. Mummy had had a bad fall in town a few days before the removal, wrenching her knee by tripping on a tram line as she hurried to catch her train home. So she was taken in the furniture van along with the furniture and carried up the two flights of stairs by the removal men, surely a first for Pickfords!

It was pretty daunting to live up two stairs in a house, where there would never be a garden to run out into. The novelty of the surroundings, however, did something to assuage my disappointment. From the bedroom at night I could hear the occasional rattle of a tramcar and at dusk I watched the lamplighter going his rounds with his long pole, igniting the gas lamps, for the side streets here had not yet been linked to the National Grid. Coal was delivered by horse and cart, the prices displayed on large cards among the coalsacks and sometimes the rag and bone man, also with horse and cart, toured hopefully calling out, "Rags, bones, and any "kinda lumba". Near Christmas the Salvation Army band played Christmas carols at the street corner, a novelty for me.

Hyndland was a well-planned area of red sandstone tenements, populated chiefly by middle-class business and professional people, and the flats varying in size from three rooms and kitchen, up to eight rooms and kitchen. The 'closes' were tiled in pale green, the rooms spacious with high corniced ceilings and large windows, many orioled. There were fine wooden features in mantelpieces, cupboards, and in some flats touches of Art Nouveau décor, such as the small stained glass windows to the side of our lounge, which benefited from being next to one of the many lanes between properties. The dining room had a dado, possibly a fashionable feature at the time of building.

Queensborough Gardens, Hyndland.

We looked out on an area of lime trees and grass, surrounded by railings. A block down was the bowling green and on warm summer evenings, with windows wide open there came the oddly soothing sound of the clicking of bowls and the rise and fall of the player's voices.

Hyndland bowling club.

The parish church which we were to attend, like the school was built in red sandstone. In this carefully planned area of West End Glasgow there were some strange gaps which in later years might have been interpreted by some as possible bomb-sites with missing houses. But no, the houses were never built and the plan never completed. As a youngster I never even thought it strange. One gap behind us made a useful short-cut to school, and once older these open areas were good places to ride around on my bicycle and meet up with pals.

In time I discovered their significance. In the late 19th century Glasgow was building many tenements to rent to middle class families. It is said that interest was lost after Lloyd George's budget of 1909, when he imposed a considerable tax on heritable property and the investors abandoned the project.

I was enrolled in the primary department of Hyndland School, not far off the close of the year and my stay there did not span a full school session. My memories of this short time are not numerous. Occasionally I saw the headmaster walk along the corridor in his black gown but his duties kept him largely in the senior school. Most, if not all teachers wore their academic gowns and I do believe it helped them to maintain authority. The lack of a gown cost one student teacher much embarrassment, I'm sure, when a long stream of pupils asked, one after another, if they could please leave the room. To my credit I did not join in this prank and I was sorry for the young man.

Being the headmaster's daughter brought me no favours however, as my class teacher soon discovered my weakness in numerical matters. One day I had a nasty fall in the playground. Falling on my head, I quickly developed a huge swelling. Instead of concern or even sympathy, she sarcastically said, "Oh, perhaps there will be a bit more space in your head now for arithmetic." I was full of resentment and never forgave her. But there was one lovely teacher who gave the girls lessons in sewing and engendered in me a love of embroidery. Some of my efforts were well worth keeping but the knickers we had to make in that sewing class were never worn! By anyone!

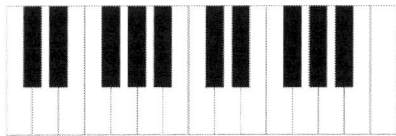

PRELUDE TO WAR

In the late 30s there had been increasing certainty of war in spite of Mr. Chamberlain's attempts for appeasement at his several meetings with Hitler. I was still happy in my childhood routine even if the adults talked much about world affairs and the wireless reports were gloomy. But I do remember quite vividly when gas-masks were issued in 1938, when we were still in Giffnock. I was made to try on this horrible black, rubber-smelling mask, which I hoped I would never have to use for real. It came in a small cardboard box with a string loop for it to be carried over your shoulder or round your neck.

By this time Anderson shelters were being erected in back gardens, so named for the Minister of Defence, Sir John Anderson. They were constructed with sheets of corrugated steel and although they might have protected people from flying debris, they would not have done much against a direct or near hit. By many they were considered to be a waste of money, although, post-war, they were still being used as useful garden sheds.

Soon Identity Cards were issued, wardens recruited for the A.R.P., air raid sirens installed, barrage balloons manufactured and appeals for men to become fire auxiliaries and women to join the W.V.S. (Women's Voluntary Service). Production of weapons, ships andaircraft was boosted, by some considered too late. It did mean fuller employment rates, the one plus point of the whole nasty business. Preparation for the possible evacuation of children from the big cities went ahead, plans of which at the time I remained quite unaware. As early as 1935 preparations for possible war were underway and even ration books, I believe, had been printed and stored well in advance. My two brothers were quite aware of the seriousness of matters and they joined the Territorial Army. On the Continent the Nazis accomplished their desired Anschlüss (Annexation of Austria) and had intensified their programme of hate against the Jewish people. At the end of 1938 came what is known in history as Kristallnacht, when on the night of November 9-10 there was systematic destruction of Jewish shops and synagogues.

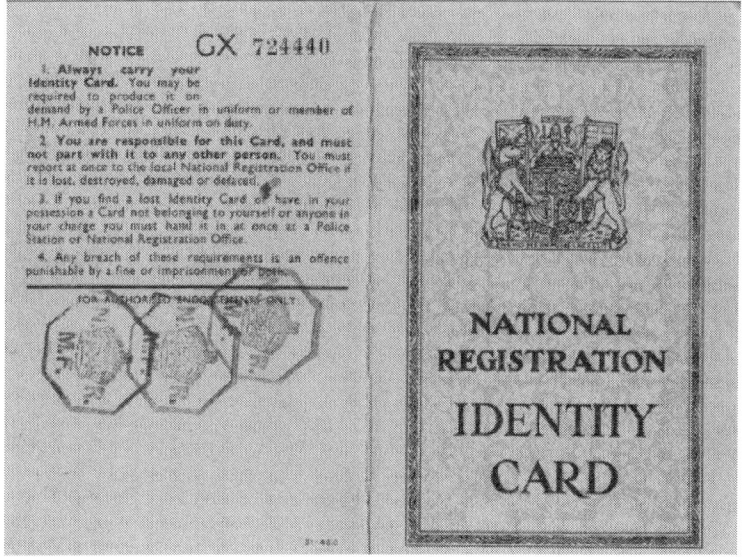

Identity card.

By March 1939 Germany had invaded Czechoslovakia. War now seemed almost inevitable.

The summer of 1939 was a lovely one and I spent my usual happy holiday on Arran, carefree in peaceful surroundings. My father had to cut short his usual long vacation to finalise arrangements for the evacuation of those of his pupils whose parents wished to take this course.

Holiday time prior to war.

Andrew and David went to summer training camp, somewhere in the Borders. My mother drove us down one day to meet them for a drive around some pretty Border countryside and lunch at a hotel, where my brothers teased me about choosing sago pudding, alias frog-spawn, from the menu for my dessert. They both hated it of course, as I already knew.

That was the last family outing. They were on the verge of serving in the army proper and in their father's old regiment of the Royal Artillery. Life was never quite the same again.

I remember when they were issued with their Dress Uniforms of the R.A. and they donned them one day for us to see. As they stood together in front of the fireplace, I was very proud of them, looking so smart in navy and red.

By the end of August, school reassembled to prepare for evacuation. On the 1st of September my mother drove Daddy and myself into the Stirlingshire countryside for him to make final arrangements at various villages. It was all confusing to me and my memory is hazy. But I do remember we drove back to Glasgow with the blackout already in force, and I was frightened, of what I hardly knew. My mother tried to reassure me and put on a brave face, although her heart must have been sore. Her husband had served in the Great War, which had claimed the life of her only brother and many young men that she had known. Now her two young sons were about to serve in yet another war.

The next day, Sept 2nd, I finally arrived in Buchlyvie, where I was to be billeted. At the school, the men and women of the village came to meet the crowd of children, and to take away their chosen ones to their new homes. Prior to the war the authorities had inspected homes and decided which would accept evacuees. I believe they often had no good reason to refuse. Because my father was headmaster to these particular children, I think my fate had been decided the day before – I was to go with the local schoolmaster, and my parents had been invited to stay over the weekend at the schoolhouse. I was the lucky one, but was more than a little puzzled when I was put into a little side room while the bustle continued beyond. And I didn't much like that there was a pickled adder in a large jar on a shelf near my head. I tried not to look! When things finally calmed down, it was time for us to go to the schoolhouse to meet Mr. Walker's wife Isa. I was given a room with a double bed, large enough to accommodate not just me, but several of my dolls and my beloved Teddy Bears.

We were introduced to the two dogs, Sandy the Cairn terrier and Tim, the fox terrier. Soon I loved them both. Sandy was a sparky little fellow, very brave in his own garden and he often barked his way up the hedge at 'intruders' on the little country road beside the schoolhouse, but not at all brave outwith his own boundaries. Tim, a very handsome chap was put out at night into his kennel beyond the backdoor, while his pal enjoyed home comforts day and night. I remember thinking that wasn't fair. Perhaps it was a matter of HIS and HERS, I don't know. Both dogs however were well cared for and well walked. The schoolhouse was a solid grey sandstone building. In the living room, where we dined except on Sundays, there was a Triplex coal-fired grate which heated the water, and in which most of the cooking was done. There was no fridge only a large larder with ventilation to the outside. The whole house was well furnished and I was lucky to have this as my temporary home. My friends Marion and Lilias were billeted respectively with the Co-op manager in their flat above the shop and with a spinster lady in a small house on the main street. The schoolhouse was a happy place and my foster parents a loving couple. He, the strict schoolmaster, used to come home, lift his slim wife up in his arms and whirl her round and round. I witnessed this often. My parents didn't indulge in such public displays of affection!

But this particular first weekend was more sombre and was, of course, of momentous historical significance. The Anglo-German Declaration which Chamberlain brought home from his meeting with Hitler in Munich in Sept. 1938, and which he famously waved in the air for the cameras, had proved worthless and now on the 3rd of Sept. 1939, his last-ditch attempts to prevent war were ignored. He came to the microphone on that lovely Sunday morning and announced to the nation, in his thin, rather high-pitched voice, that we were, "therefore now at war with Germany." I can remember that moment vividly. The die was cast and for the next six years the world was to be thrown into complete turmoil.

The village of Buchylvie lies on the line of the old military road linking Dumbarton and Stirling, built on General Wade's orders after the Jacobite rebellion. When I knew it as a child, it consisted largely of a long straight street with a couple of pubs ('The Red Lion' and 'The Black Bull') and several shops, two butchers, a grocers, post office, saddlers, and a Co-op store. Approaching the village from the Balfron end one came first to the distinctive village hall, its four-sided clock tower topped by a dome. The schoolhouse lay practically opposite and the evening chimes of 9 o'clock came to signal 'bedtime' for me. At the opposite end of the main street lay the South church and war memorial. It was to this church, built in 1835, that I was taken to morning service on Sundays. Mr. Walker, a very important man in the village, was Session Clerk here and choirmaster, duties that he performed with others, such as director of Amateur Dramatics and leader of more than one village club.

Running down at right angles from the main street was Station road, where the two-teacher school lay and also the North church which had originally been the United Presbyterian place of worship, and its manse. Close to the school was the 'sweetie' shop, very convenient for the children of the village. A bell rang when we opened the door, alerting the lady shopkeeper to come from the back shop, usually attired in a floral pinafore. On the shelves behind her were large glass jars filled with brightly coloured sweets – cinnamon balls, soor-plooms, black-striped balls, liquorice allsorts, toffees. On the counter lay boxes of Cowan's Highland Toffee bars, pink-tipped sugar cigarettes, liquorice straps, chewing gum, sugar mice, sherbet and chocolate buttons. Before the introduction of rationing of confectionary, we were able to purchase sweets for a half-penny, something like a gobstopper for a farthing. To spend a whole penny at once was extravagant indeed. We could buy 'scraps' here too and marbles, and at Halloween, false faces.

Buchlyvie.

Just before Halloween, coming back from church, some boys were spotted in a swede field, pinching some for 'lanterns'. Mr Walker commented on it and I said, "Oh, the buggers". Of course I was severely reprimanded for using such a word.

Station road did lead to the station, where trains ran along the Blane Valley line to Glasgow, till it finally closed in 1950. It being a distance from the village, most people found Alexander's Bluebird buses more convenient for travel between Glasgow and Stirling, and beyond.

Further down this road lay damp marshy ground, the outer limit of the large Flanders Moss. In Spring we children came down here to witness large numbers of frogs on their way to their spawning grounds. Such large numbers that even in these days of few cars, many got squashed. The boys found eels here too and we were organised early in the war to collect Sphagnum moss for the 'war effort'. It was still used, as it had been in the Great War, as dressings for wounds. Black-headed gulls nested in noisy colonies down here on the moss and some of the boys collected eggs for eating, something I never experienced.

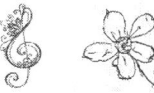

Flanders Moss was part of a huge area of bog-land that at one time had stretched for miles towards Stirling, and in early times proved to be an unsurmountable barrier for both man and horse. No crossing of the infant Forth was possible between what was known as the Fords of Frew near Aberfoyle and Stirling itself. In the 18th century however, much draining was undertaken by improving landlords, known as the Moss Lairds, thus converting many acres into rich farmland. Two such moss-lairds were one Archibald Napier and Andrew Graham, second son of the then Duke of Montrose, who laid out the villages of Thornhill and Buchlyvie respectively.

The nearest village to Buchlyvie is Arnprior from where a road leads to the Lake of Mentieth, the site of past 'Bonspiels'. The last of these I believe took place in 1979. With global warming perhaps there will never be another. On the Lake of Menteith lies the island of Inchmahome with its ruined priory, the 'island of rest', as indeed it was for R.B. Cunninghame Graham, one of the founders of the Labour Party, who is buried here. The priory had, much earlier been at one time, a refuge for Queen Mary of Scots. One of the many explanations of the strange name of Flanders is that the Augustinian monks at the priory came from Flanders. Arnprior's name makes good sense as 'Arn' means a portion, and it would have been part of the priory's lands.

The Moss itself, one of the largest raised bogs in Europe, has thankfully, but in much reduced form, been preserved because of its outstanding environmental interest. Botanists visit still to study the flora and to see the rare Ledum (Labrador tea) and other bog plants like sundews, cranberry and bog rosemary growing among the sphagnum mosses. The improved area, the Carse of Stirling, has been noted for fine crops and grassland, supporting cattle and horses, and where flocks of geese graze in winter or fly over in their spectacular V-shaped formations.

Sundew.

The Andrew Graham, founder of Buchlyvie, was possibly also known as the Baron of Buchlyvie, a title that goes back as far as the 16th century. After my evacuation to Buchlyvie, I remember my father reciting with great amusement a rhyme which was quoted in Sir Walter Scott's 'Rob Roy' and which runs thus:-

'Baron of Bucklivie,

May the foul fiend drive ye,

And a' to pieces rive ye,

For building sic a town,

Where there's neither horse-meat, nor man's meat,

nor a chair to sit down.'

A famous stallion named Baron of Buchlyvie was bred in the area and was sold for the colossal sum of £9,500 sometime before its demise at the beginning of the 20th century. So famous was it that the Glasgow Art Galleries and Museum thought it worthwhile to purchase his skeleton for public display.

'Rob Roy', Scott's famous novel, was part fact and part fiction but much of it was set in the Aberfoyle and Trossachs area, which is not many miles beyond Buchlyvie. From the village we could look over towards Ben Venue and Ben Ledi, and other high ground of the Trossachs.

But as a child my life in the village was largely spent on home territory, at school and the schoolhouse and as much time as possible outdoors with my pals. A side road, Culbowie Road, climbed up beyond the schoolhouse between lush hedges and up to a patch of woodland where we collected hazelnuts in autumn, took turns on a sledge in winter, learned to eat young hawthorn leaves and search for birds' nests in springtime. The bird-nesting was done in the company of Jimmy. He and I had exchanged 'love notes' in the classroom. One of these was intercepted by the schoolmaster and I'm sure he didn't know what to do about it! In his wisdom he ignored it and no harm was done, and the bird-nesting continued.

My two special friends who had come from Hyndland and the other girls of the village were always busy with skipping ropes, ball games, and playing 'peever' (hopscotch) its lines chalked on the village pavements, and sometimes we played hide and seek with the boys, or Rounders in the field behind the school. I had a craze for roller-skates and with the village almost traffic-free it was a fairly safe occupation, even going down the hill at speed to the school.

In the winter of 1940 there was a severe spell of weather and Jack Frost visited my bedroom window, leaving elaborate patterns of fronds and leaves. Even from the inside, I had to scrape with my fingernails to clear patches to look out. No central heating then! One morning Mr. Walker opened the back door to find himself faced with a huge wall of snow and some hard digging was required for us to get out. In such weather the school carried on and even the children from outlying farms made it, even if a little late. Never a possibility of the school being closed as would possibly happen today. Yet, it **was** cold and I was glad of my Chilprufe vest and Liberty bodice!

The snow lasted long enough for me to experience sledging for the first time, on high ground behind the village. A boy a few years older than me and who was already a pupil at the senior school at Balfron, for some reason befriended me and allowed me to share his sledge. I felt very honoured. Ian who lived with his parents in a house on the main street befriended me further, even allowing me into the inner sanctum of his bedroom, where he kept a time-table pinned up on his wall, with his days all mapped out for his various interests. He was a budding pianist, quite advanced and hours of practice were carefully planned. In later years, thinking this approach to life had much to recommend it, I tried briefly. But no, I didn't have the will power to continue with it for long, although still later I came across a book, by Arnold Bennet, 'How to Live 24 Hours a Day'. Again I flirted with the idea briefly.

In early summer a small conical hill opposite the church was covered with bluebells and the girls picked bunches here. In autumn a magnificent horse chestnut tree beyond the other end of the village became the focus of attention for the boys in particular, as they chose the largest of the nuts, polished like fine furniture. Conkers became the temporary rage.

While playing hide and seek, or just pottering about in odd corners of the village, a group of us found ourselves one day in the lane behind the butchers where the small local slaughter house lay. That day we heard the shot, and in a second or so the animal fell to the floor, a scene very disturbing to a child. The picture of it remains in my mind to this day.

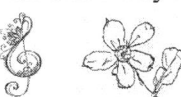

War didn't touch the children too much except when a convoy of army trucks passed through the village and we waved enthusiastically to the soldiers, or when we heard aircraft overhead. Unknown to us at the time, the woodlands around Aberfoyle were used to conceal large stores of live ammunition. Possibly the small convoys of trucks that we often saw were coming from or going to these stores, housed in Nissan huts.

Our 'war effort' was confined to knitting squares for blankets and socks for the forces, and under supervision, collecting Sphagnum moss, and in autumn, rose-hips from the hedges. These, so rich in vitamin C, were collected for the manufacture of the National Rose-hip Syrup. And of course along with the adults, wartime children had to accept the rationing of food. The boys chalked swastikas and moustached Hitler faces on walls and pavements, not out of admiration, rather by way of mockery and hatred. We were well aware of some of what was going on in the world through the wireless, which was listened to religiously throughout the nation.

Rose-hips

On the lighter side of course, there were the well-known and much sung wartime favourites like "We'll Hang Out the Washing on the Siegfried Line", "Run Rabbit Run", "Roll out the Barrel", Vera Lynn's "White Cliffs of Dover", and "We'll Meet Again", and later the ridiculous "Mairzy Doats and Dozy Doats and a Liddle Lamzy Divey". This immensely popular ditty could be translated, if so wished, into "Mares Eat Oats and Does Eat Oats and Little Lambs Eat Ivy". One wartime saying that caught on with the children and was often repeated while playing games – "Halt Who Goes There?"

Early in the war, the Government launched a campaign to encourage people to grow their own vegetables. The country during the 20s and 30s had relied heavily on imported food, from Canadian and U.S. wheat and New Zealand lamb and butter, to South African fruit and even vegetables from the continent. Convoys of merchant ships were at risk from U-boat attack and food shortages were expected. The campaign became known as "Dig for Victory" and even lawns, playing fields, ornamental gardens were dug up all over the country, even at stately homes such as Kensington Palace. Allotments were established in many towns, and lots of Government leaflets were produced, telling people how to cultivate their patches, when to sow or plant, and what crops to grow.

Along with the Dig for Victory campaign the Autumn Potato Holiday arrived, when school pupils were used to help at the tattie lifting. I was too young to take part but in the Autumn of 1940 and with the schools closed, it allowed for a week's holiday with Mummy and Daddy at Corrie on Arran. We stayed in one of the whitewashed cottages which line the road here just above the shore. I pottered about a lot near the old stone harbour, finding enough sand to make sand-pies and I went brambling with Mummy.

Snowdrops.

In Buchlyvie Mr. Walker organised the boys to dig up a patch near the back of the school and he put most of his own back garden over to vegetables – leeks and onions, potatoes and cabbage, and small patches of lettuce and parsley. Naturally there was competition in the village to see who could grow the biggest, fattest and finest. To the side of the schoolhouse there were two plum trees which produced so much fruit one year, the whole school was invited to partake. In the front garden I remember the serried rows of snowdrops in early spring and clumps of sweet-smelling Phlox in late summer.

In the early months of the war, Saturdays meant a visit to Falkirk where both Mr and Mrs. Walker had been brought up and where they had relations. After lunch we would set off in the green Hillman car, out of the village, following the road which marks the southern edge of the fertile Carse of Stirling. We passed the entrance to Garden Mansion, at that time home to Sir Steven Bilsland, the District Commissioner for Civil Defence in the Glasgow area. A dozen or so lucky evacuees had been billeted here.

Beyond Arnprior we came through the village of Kippen, made famous by its huge vine. Two Buchanan brothers had established a market garden here and, between the wars, had built up a successful business, selling flowers, fruit and vegetables widely. Duncan Buchanan was well-trained in horticulture and had been head gardener at the lovely Culzean Estate on the Ayrshire Coast. But what brought him fame was the Gros Colman vine, which in growth had outstripped all expectations, eventually covering about 5,000 square metres and producing up to 2000 bunches in a season. These, and grapes from other vines were sold to quality markets even as far away as London. But on our Saturday outing this famous spot was passed as we drove by Gargunnock to Stirling itself, the old Castle towering above the low ground. The roads were quiet, but even so Mr. Walker's temper was easily ruffled by bad drivers and he would sometimes wind down his window to shout at them!

The visits to Falkirk were often so that Mr. Walker could go to support his football club, at a home match. I was left with Mrs. Walker. At one house we often visited I would be taken out the back to visit the pigeon loft, with a keen pigeon fancier. Here I was able to admire his beauties at close quarters, seeing their plumage of greys, whites, and purples with sparkles of green while they purred "drroouu" contentedly.

Once football was over we would go to a restaurant for high tea. Fish was a highlight, but the cakes served on three-tiered cake stands were not exciting in wartime. I remember shiny round cookies meant to look tempting but filled with ersatz cream which I found rather repulsive! Weekends with no 'at home' game, usually meant a visit to the cinema – called either the pictures or the flicks in these days. I don't know what films we saw but I did know that Dianne Durban was Mr. Walker's pin-up girl at the time. There was always a Pathé news bulletin where war developments and news were reported in the fast, clipped tones customary with reporters of the time.

The car journey back to Buchlyvie in the black out was slow and I was often lulled to sleep in the back seat by the hum of the engine and the warmth of the travelling rug in which I was wrapped – a necessary item in every car before such undreamt-of luxuries as car heaters. And so to bed, with church and a quiet Sunday ahead, and back to school on Monday morning.

The village school of grey sandstone was a two-teacher one where all classes from infants to the Qualifying class were managed by two teachers, Mr. Walker supervising in the senior room, Miss Cowie in the junior one. As the school population had increased with the evacuees, I have memories of a relief teacher helping out. She was a bit dolled-up and unused to Spartan village life and tried to spend as much time as possible blocking out the heat from the coal fire in the corner of the room.

The local children, some from outlying farms, and the incomers integrated well and I don't remember any friction or jealousy on either side. It was a happy place and so too was the playground where boys and girls played together. No bullying, no fights.

On the walls of the junior room there were big posters of the world, at that time so much of it in red, marking the enormity of the British Empire. We were ignorant of the divisions within it and that the cracks appearing would in a few years' time lead to its final disintegration and the emergence instead of a Commonwealth of Nations.

In this room we were taught spelling, arithmetic, bits of geography, and history. There were knitting and sewing sessions for the girls and we learned some songs with Miss Cowie at the piano. My favourites were "Cherry Ripe" and "All Through the Night".

Once into the senior room I found out that Mr Walker, who at home was kindly, jovial and always understanding, was now the strict teacher with a leather strap handy, ready for use if deemed necessary. I enjoyed no special treatment and did on one occasion receive the whack of the leather. Mental arithmetic was my bête noire and I dreaded the daily session of this. Yet when I fell short I sometimes thought there was a kindly twinkle of understanding in his eye.

There were some highlights to school life, as when we went to the village hall, our numbers boosted by pupils from other local schools, for a performance by Bertha Waddell's Children's Theatre. It toured all around the country at that time and I remember being at another performance later in Glasgow. Miss Waddell herself always introduced the song and dance show by poking her head between the stage curtains and calling, "Hello children".

The village hall was well-used, even in wartime, with Amateur dramatics, meetings, dances, and occasional film-shows. From my bedroom I sometimes heard chatter and laughter as people dispersed to make their way home.

On occasions when my foster-parents were off on an evening, I never knew where, I would spend the time with Miss Cowie at the North manse where she would play board games with me and allow me to rummage through a wardrobe and a large trunk where lots of clothes and costumes were kept for use in the local amateur dramatics. Some dressing up was allowed here and it was great fun. Amateur Dramatics were very much alive and well in the villages of Stirlingshire at this time.

Occasionally I would be left in the charge of the Co-op manager and his wife where my best pal of the time, Marion, was billeted. It was a novelty to imagine life 'above the shop' and here lovely cups of cocoa were served instead of my usual evening Horlicks.

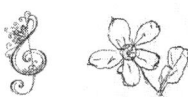

The early months of the war were full of expectation but nothing much seemed to be happening – the Phoney War, as it came to be known. It lulled many into a false sense of calm and security, including my parents, who thought it might be perfectly safe for me to return to Glasgow on some weekends, ostensibly for piano lessons.

At the end of such weekends my mother would see me on Monday morning onto the Stirling bus early enough for me to arrive in Buchlyvie for school opening. The cream and blue bus with its 'Bluebird' on the side would then run out of Glasgow by Milngavie and Strathblane, round the base of the Campsie Fells, and below the volcanic plug of Dumgoyne, a well-known landmark visible from many parts of the city and regarded with affection even by the majority who never climbed it. Just beyond it, the bus passed the sizeable village of Killearn. It was here, still in the shadow of Dumgoyne that an emergency hospital was built early in the war and where many victims of the Clydebank blitz of 1941 were treated.

Further on the bus reached Balfron which had the secondary school, taking its pupils from the surrounding villages. Balfron's most famous son was Alexander 'Greek' Thomson, the well-known architect whose fondness for the Classical style earned him his name. He stamped his mark on a number of much admired Glasgow buildings, notably his churches. My father told the story of a passer-by looking up at the Greek pillars of one of

Thompson's churches and asking a cleaner sweeping the steps – "And what God do they worship here?"

Balfron's main thoroughfare was Buchanan Street, as the chief land-owners of this area were of that name. The name of the nearby settlement of Boquan is, I believe, a vernacular version of Buchanan. The Endrick River, a fine trout fishing stream, flows through this same area and meanders in loops and bends over low-lying ground, to reach Loch Lomond below Buchanan Castle. Four miles or so beyond Balfron and I was back at school.

During one very severe spell of weather, with heavy snowfalls, the buses couldn't run and I had my weekend visit to Glasgow extended for a day or two till the roads were cleared. Not cleared in the sense we know that word today with our snowploughs and road-salt, but literally dug out. When finally I was able to board a bus for Buchlyvie, it ran in places between great walls of snow on either side that I couldn't see over.

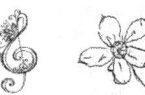

During some delightful summery weather in May 1940 I suddenly fell ill with mumps. I think there may have been panic in the village and Mr Walker feared the school might experience an epidemic. Miraculously I was the sole victim and it was concluded that I must have contracted it on one of my Glasgow visits.

Suddenly I got the VIP treatment and after the initial discomfort and indisposition it was nice to be molly-coddled. Somebody sent flowers and my sledging friend Ian sent books and puzzles via his mother. I now had time to read 'Black Beauty' and 'Treasure Island', and was introduced to the little Glasgow character 'Wee MacGreegor' in J.J.Bell's book of the 20s.

My mother was summoned to help out one weekend while the Walkers went to Falkirk, and in spite of doctor's orders that I was to stay in bed, she got me seated outside wrapped up to enjoy the sunshine and the garden.

One lovely day, myself now recovered, but not yet back to school she came with my brother Andrew to collect me and we drove over to Aberfoyle and Loch Ard. At the beautiful Foresthills Hotel, long since a Time-share property, we were served luncheon at a window table overlooking trees, the loch, and the hills beyond, which separate Loch Ard from Loch Lomond. Afterwards we pottered by the shore and in the woods, a lovely interlude, no doubt for Andrew as well, home on leave.

Andrew, on leave.

ARGYLL

By now the Phoney War was no longer. In April the Germans invaded Denmark and Norway and soon Belgium, Holland, and France. The B.E.F. and the French armies were making little headway against the enemy and late May and early June saw the retreat from Dunkirk, when thousands of 'little ships' – fishing boats, yachts, small motor vessels – crossed the Channel to help in the rescue of as many troops as they possibly could. Although Dunkirk was a full scale retreat it was in some ways seen almost as a victory. News bulletins and the papers were full of it and everybody – even the children – were well aware of it.

Chamberlain resigned and Winston Churchill was asked to form a national government with ministers from both sides of the political spectrum. With party political differences cast aside they set to work together with one aim. The Allies soon had to retreat from Norway and both King Haakon of Norway and Queen Willhelmina of the Netherlands sought refuge in the U.K., as did the leaders of other European nations.

By June the Nazis had invaded the Channel Isles and there was real fear that Hitler's troops would invade along the coast of southern England. As 1940 progressed the outlook was grim and Churchill sought to inspire the nation with his stirring and defiant speeches listened to by everyone. The 9 o'clock news was a daily rallying point.

In spite of the seriousness of the war now, my parents were already considering my possible return to Glasgow to school there, and they did consider a couple of boarding schools, but that came to nothing. There had been a serious offer from some of my mother's Canadian relations to have me to stay there for the duration of the war. The offer had been declined, although many children did cross the Atlantic to seek safety; but tragedy struck when the ship City of Benaras was sunk by a U boat on her way to Canada in September 1940. Almost a hundred of the evacuees on board were drowned.

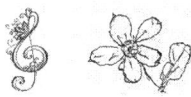

But during that first summer of the war, my mother having been called south to help Aunt Winnie nurse her husband through an illness, the usual Arran holiday was cancelled and I was sent up to stay with the kindly folk on Loch Aweside, where I spent two wonderful months running wild and learning more of the countryside and farming life.

Since the first family visit here at Easter 1938 there had been several more and would be many more right up to my University days and at different times of the year.

There were two ways to go. If enough petrol had been saved up, we could drive up the side of the lovely Loch Lomond, through Colquhoun country and the little hamlet of Luss, in later years the location used for the TV series 'The High Road', up to Tarbet (the Isthmus) and across the narrow neck of land to Loch Long, with Arrochar at its head. Daddy always reminisced here about his climbs of the Cobbler (Ben Arthur) in former days. Up now the steep, tortuous hill-climb to the Rest and Be Thankful. In these days it was a challenge for both car and driver, but has long since been widened, straightened and improved, and affords an easy run down to Loch Fyne, which I came to know much better as an adult.

Loch Fyne, a long sea-arm from the Firth of Clyde was of course at one time a busy centre of the long-lost herring industry. Once down from the high ground we would round the head of Loch Fyne, passing the ruin of Dunderave Castle on its green, grassy waterside site. This was the castle depicted as "Doom Castle" by Neil Munro in his novel of that name. This is true Neil Munro country, for here at the county town of Inveraray he was born in 1864, although much of his life as a writer was spent in Glasgow. His novels such as "The New Road", and "John Splendid" were still popular in the 30s and 40s and of course his wonderful Para Handy tales have lived on, even on screen.

Beyond Inveraray the road climbs up through lovely Glen Aray and at the tiny hamlet of Cladich, the junction there marks the start of the journey down Loch Aweside for the motorist.

During the war, with petrol rationed, our journey was oftener by train to Dalmally, where Mr Crawford would meet us in his Ford car. The train ran to Stirling and Dunblane, where near the station stood the cathedral and my father would tell me of the Victoria School here, which had been founded to give education to children of soldiers, perhaps those that had fallen in the Boer War and the Great War. The railway line ran through beautiful countryside by Doune and Callender and beyond. I have memories of masses of bird cherry trees in blossom here in Springtime. The line has long since been closed but it was a single track and at each station – Strathyre, Lochearnhead, and all the others, the so-called 'tablet' had to be exchanged between driver and stationmaster. To me it

looked like a solid leather wallet with a huge metal ring on it. Only
with the appropriate tablet in his possession was it safe for the driver to proceed. My father, who was always good at imparting
knowledge in a delightfully informal way, explained all this to his
small daughter, and as the train left the more benign countryside
behind, to climb up through the lonely Glen Ogle, he would allow
me to stick my head out of the lowered window to watch the engine
puffing out much smoke as it wound its way round a viaduct ahead.
Then it was down by Crianlarich and Tyndrum to Dalmally.

The upper part of Loch Awe is studded with small islands, with
the bulk of Ben Cruachan standing sentinel at its head. Later the big
power station would be built into its bowels, a wonder of engineer-
ing at the height of hydroelectricity development in Scotland. The
much-photographed Kilchurn Castle, often appearing in calendars
and magazines used to stand on an island, but it is now on a grassy
area, damp constantly, by the lochside. This was once a stronghold
of the Campbell clan.

For most of its twenty-odd mile length the loch is narrow, often
much less than a mile across. Before the war a pleasure steamer had
plied these waters in the same way as one still does on Loch Lomond and Loch Katrine but I never saw that. I know I am probably
biased, but surely Loch Awe must be one of the most beautiful
stretches of fresh water in all Scotland. Along its southern shore a
single track road at times ran close to the water.

It was a perfect fairyland of birch, oak, alder, and willow woodland with ditches and banks lush with ferns and wild flowers.
Glimpses of the opposite shore were seen when there were gaps in
the lochside woodland. Such gaps sometimes revealed a gravelly

shoreline and sparkling water, sometimes a bed of wild irises or a small grove of bog myrtle.

Loch Awe.

Loch Awe.

Bog myrtle.

A few miles along this road we passed the Sonachan Hotel, a favourite resort of anglers. And in another few miles we came to Blarghour, in an open area, the farmhouse sitting high above the road. Its Gaelic name can be translated as 'the clearing of the goat', but if there were wild goats here at one time, there was no word of them now, although in these early times of mine here, there had been relatively recent sightings of the wild cat.

Blarghour farmhouse.

So it was here for that early wartime summer that I was taken into the farm family and treated as one of their own, running about with the farm children around the steading, the fields, the moorland, and the lochside. I loved it and was very happy.

Blarghour was a sheep farm where blackface sheep roamed over a big area of high ground, between Loch Awe itself and towards Loch Fyne. And there were hardy Galloway cattle too who spent their lives out of doors on the high ground, and a couple of milking cows to supply the family and guests with milk and cream, and for the butter-making. Hens scratched around free-range, safe to roam where they wished. And there were always the border-collies, cats, and kittens. The cats were farm cats, living in the barn or hayshed, except for one spoilt lady – a black feline who rejoiced in the unimaginative name of Kitty. She spent lots of her time in the kitchen and often lay as close as she could to the Rayburn cooker, while the others had to be content with their meals on the doorstep!

The farm was run by Mr Crawford, his shepherd, Donald, and with help from the boys as they grew up. The shepherd's cottage stood up behind the farmhouse by the edge of the moorland where, in season, the silky heads of cotton grass shivered in the breeze, among heather and moorland grasses.

The shepherd's cottage.

As Donald was a bachelor, he chose to lodge with the family. The cottage was occupied one year by the naturalist and author, Richard Perry, who being a conscientious objector, chose to work on farms, and at the same time was able to observe wildlife and do his writing. While I was there two agricultural students, gaining practical experience, increased the size of the family that sat down to meals at the big kitchen table. Sometimes they joined in sing-songs round the piano, and composed silly rhymes and did a lot of teasing of Mary and myself. Donald spent some of his spare time quietly carving away at sheep horns into forms to decorate the tops of shepherd's crooks.

On important days in the sheep-farming calendar, shepherds from other farms would come to help and they would enjoy a large midday meal in the kitchen, before returning to an afternoon of work. One such day was the one known as the 'clipping' (the shearing). I watched, fascinated as the men, seated on stools with each succeeding animal held firmly between their knees as they deftly removed the fleece in the old-fashioned way, with hand-shears. Afterwards the fleeces would be rolled, tied and stored high in piles in the big barn to await eventual uplift by lorry. We children made ourselves useful by opening and shutting gates between pens, for of course the ewes were separated from their lambs, the mothers themselves only being released for clipping one at a time and then put into another pen before finally being allowed to join their offspring. There was much noise and bustle but I soon enjoyed the sound and smell of sheep.

Over time I picked up the terms used for different ages and types. The blackface tups were fine looking fellows with their curly horns, but just a touch scary if they came too close. The more docile ewes of course had lambs at foot. Hogs were year-old lambs and gimmers, into their second year, would be put in lamb by the end of the year, at the 'tupping' – a time of year I was never here. Nor was I, aged nine, much concerned with the sex-life of sheep. Unfortunately there are always losses at lambing time. Orphan lambs can sometimes be adopted by another ewe, if temporarily covered in her dead lamb's coat. If all else fails there may be lambs that are bottle-fed, and it so happened in that happy summer that Mary, literally, had a little lamb, which would follow her around the steading, skipping and prancing happily by her side. Occasionally I was allowed to give it its bottle – a great thrill for me.

Duncan & Rosalind with pet lamb.

Haymaking was of course another big event on the farm, but more of a family affair than the clipping and the dipping. The children were fully involved. Unlike the method in Arran, where most of the hay was left in ricks in the stackyard, here, once finally dried to satisfaction, the ricks were brought in and the hay safely stored in the huge metal hayshed, where, as children, Duncan and I climbed and tumbled about and where the odd broody hen would lay eggs or a cat have her kittens.

Donald, the shepherd, spent most of his time out on the hill, but on really wet days on the farm, he joined in the main scene of activity at the open-fronted woodshed, where log after log would be sawn with a two-handled cross-cut saw, the rhythmic sound of it changing as the log was penetrated, finally to fall with a soft thud into the accumulating pile of sawdust. We learned how to stack these logs into a neat pile against the back wall of the woodshed. Quite a lot of alder was cut and it seemed to make a good fire. I was never witness to the felling of wood, but I believe it was judiciously done and the natural birch and alder woodland rejuvenated itself well.

In the morning there was the fun of collecting eggs to take back to the larder. And in the evenings, after milking time, Duncan and I, the youngest, would be allowed to see the cows back into their pasture and trusted to see that the gate was firmly closed. An area of this pasture was damp with tiny pools among rushes and here we sometimes lingered to watch huge blue dragonflies hover and dart and swallows swoop and whirl overhead.

On the opposite side of the steading another drier, grassy area lay between farm and burn, with many rabbit burrows and runs. Here I sometimes accompanied the boys as they set snares on these runs. In later life it is not a practice I would have approved of, but with hindsight I can see that a country family, miles from any shop and with wartime food rationing in place, would be pleased to get something 'for the pot'. The snares would have been inspected I've no doubt before I was abroad of a morning.

Judging by the only occasional appearance of rabbit on the menu, I don't think all that many were trapped. But on the first occasion that it was cooked for dinner during my stay, a trick was played on me. Having stated that I didn't like rabbit (my mother's cooking of this once had not been relished by me) Daddy Crawford, as I thought of him now, was serving up at the head of the table, when Mrs C. told him that that piece of chicken to the side was for Rosalind. Only after I had cleared my plate was I asked if that had been nice and then was informed that it was rabbit! That cured me!

The local laird occasionally sent a gift of salmon and, I believe, in season a brace of pheasant for the menu. The brown trout caught by the boys near the mouth of the burn were always relished, and Donald sometimes shot a mountain hare on the hill, as these were numerous here in these bygone days.

Above the farm the Blarghour burn falls in spectacular manner down its ninety-foot waterfall, but it was benign and calm as it reached the loch's edge, among willows and alders, and where the lovely globe flower flourished. In later years the Blarghour Falls were harnessed to generate electricity for the farm, but for the moment that was in the future.

Blarghour Falls.

The sloping garden to the front of the house was not large, but supplied a remarkable amount of produce, vegetables, some fruit and flowers. A summer visit to Mrs C's old home near Inveraray allowed us to pick gooseberries, raspberries, and strawberries to supplement the diet, and to make jam.

It was here, at this large farm a few years later that my father, mother and myself were invited to join in a Christmas tradition, where the farm hands joined the family at the kitchen table for a Christmas Eve meal, the highlight of which was the huge clootie dumpling divided up and served with fresh cream.

Saturday evenings back at Blarghour had two fixed events. One was the 'Saturday van', the only provisions van that came this length and only once a week, so there was much carrying of goods into the larder or the kitchen with the essentials for the coming week. The other fixed event was the wireless programme of Scottish dance music. Many of the traditional tunes I learnt here, some with unforgettable names such as "The Mucking o' Geordie's Byre", "The Deil Amang the Tailors", and "The Braes of Tulliemet". Even at an early age, the two boys were learning to play the accordion and the fiddle. Their mother was musical, playing the piano, and sometimes the organ in the tiny church further up the lochside.

On Sunday mornings, if there was no service to be held, either at the little church or in the local schoolroom, Daddy Crawford would gather everyone together for short Bible readings, a prayer and a couple of hymns with piano accompaniment.

In that early summer I learned to run about barefoot, emulating Duncan, who already had toughened soles to his feet. To begin with it could be decidedly uncomfortable but I persevered and eventually we ran about the steading together, into the fields or up the little hazel-wooded fairy knoll which lay to one side of the house, and from where a tawny owl sometimes hooted at night. We even made it barefoot down to the loch to paddle. There was a craze for stilts – I don't remember who made or brought them for us, but it was great fun walking tall. The family pet, a Cairn terrier called Curach, often ran about with us. The road was so quiet at that time there would hardly be a car pass in a day. The local roadman worked his way up from his home a mile or more away, scything road edges and clearing ditches, and returning home again by bicycle. The postman was the only regular, conveying letters and parcels in his red van, and uplifting any mail to be posted. On the odd occasion that another vehicle was heard on the road, its sound was picked up at once by Curach, who would bark excitedly, sending Mary flying to the front door to see if she knew who it was!

Petrol, being precious, the car was only taken out occasionally, and to reach the last call of the butcher's van somebody would be dispatched by bicycle to await his arrival at the next farm community, to collect the week's rations of meat and sausages.

Once the car went up to Sonachan where we crossed the loch to attend a sale of work at Taycreggan. The small ferry boat was summoned by ringing a bell at the little jetty below the hotel. Country sales of work were occasions for meeting other people and making purchases of jam, home-baking, vegetables, summer fruit, knitted socks or jerseys and various knick-knacks. Sales of work were of no interest to the boys so this excursion was only for Mrs

C., Mary, and myself. To me the most exciting part, of course, was the crossing of the loch. Back home the jars of jam and chutneys would be placed on a shelf in the larder.

Next to the larder lay the stone-floored dairy where large shallow basins of milk were left over days to sour, before being put into the wooden churn for the butter-making. Hard, hard turning of the churn handle eventually produced lumps of butter. It was a long tedious process, followed by much washing and rewashing. It was all a bit boring to me – I preferred to be outdoors – but Mary, always helping her mother in domestic duties, I think may even then, in her early teens, been the chief butter-maker. Finally it was ready to be moulded into shape with wooden butter pats. For the table rounds of butter might have a thistle pattern on the top, or on occasions butter-balls were presented, always served with a butter knife, for guests.

Down in the lochside boathouse lay the boat that was used by angling guests, but also by the family. Mary and Ernest could both row reasonably well and were allowed to do so on occasions. No doubt modern health and safety officials would be horrified at such behaviour. However, these were the old days, when children were allowed freedom to learn by experience and sometimes by their mistakes. A picnic outing was planned by the four of us and one afternoon we set off, plus dog, in the boat with our picnic safely stowed in its basket under one of the seats, to row down the loch to the island of Innis Chonnel, which lay out from the tiny hamlet of Portinisherrich. In the early days it still had its post office, where sweets and postcards could be bought. On Innis Chonnel lie the ruins of a castle, an old fortress of the Campbells.

Innis Chonnel.

Once we reached the island and the boat was secured, we ran about, exploring the ivy clad ruins, playing hide and seek, and skimming stones across the water. A spooky heron rose on giant wings, barking at our intrusion and we disturbed a duck with her little flotilla of ducklings. Curach joined in the fun. After the picnic, Mary noticed that the wind was rising a little and she thought that we should think of going home. All too soon we were back on the water. With the rising wind it was ruffled into little waves, then the waves very quickly got bigger and bigger. It must have been hard rowing, as the boat finally moved up and down, as if on the sea. Before we made it back to the boathouse, poor Curach was getting distressed and finally was a little 'seasick'. Once safely back on dry land we felt very pleased with ourselves, the dog now recovered and prancing by our feet. Other boat outings followed along the little bays of the loch, some of which bore names given to them by ourselves, but this outing was the highlight. What freedom, what fun!

On another occasion there was an expedition to Kilmartin, I presume for supplies of some kind, but I was taken along, motoring down passed the estate of Eredine with its fringe of dark Rhododendrons and by Ford, the village at the south western end of Loch Awe, and into the district of Kilmartin, an area rich in prehistoric sites. Here cairns, standing stones, and rock carvings abound. This was all rather beyond me at the time but Mrs Crawford, interested in such things suggested that we should go that little bit further to Kilmichael Glassary and took us up the hill of Dunadd, believed to be the crowning place of the first King of Dalriada in the fourth century. Here the famous footprint in the rock was shown to us and here the nation of Scotland was born, so we were told.

But in childhood holiday mode, education, if any was only picked up in the passing, and we were more bent on fun. More than once, thistles and stones were stuffed down my bed and I discovered that prickly burdock heads, with a hen's feather inserted, made a fine weapon to attack from the rear! On wet days we played board games indoors, Chinese checkers and Monopoly. In fact we became completely obsessed with the latter and never tired of it. Wet days could be fun too.

Country folks are usually very sociable, although their neighbours may be several miles apart. One evening there was a gathering in the kitchen of friends and neighbours, with much chat and laughter, plenty food and tea, and a glass or two for the adults, plus Scottish dance music on somebody's accordion. A ceilidh in fact – the first and only one which I ever attended. It meant a late night to bed, but who cared about that?

On over the war years and beyond, right up to my university days my parents and I returned here for holidays. We all loved the peace and quiet of the unspoiled countryside and the friendship of the family. Father loved his days out fishing, sometimes from the shore, but often from the boat, with my mother rowing, until I was old enough to be entrusted with the oars. I enjoyed this and as the years passed, became quite efficient at it, rowing Father along into little bays and corners of the lochside where he thought his luck might be in, and where I had to hold the boat at rest while he cast his line.

But there was fishing from the shore too, and here I learned the art of dry-fly fishing, where one threw the line out from the spinning reel at speed, landing the fly on the surface of the water. This appealed to me more than other forms of fishing, and soon I could cast my line out a considerable distance, almost as far as Daddy.

But now however, as I grew older, the world of plants became my real passion. It was while fishing that I first saw the root nodules of an alder tree, where high levels of water had washed them clean of soil. Subsequently I discovered that these nodules were able to fix nitrogen from the atmosphere. And here too were fluffy pussy catkins on the willows in springtime and the small tight catkins of the sweet-smelling bog myrtle.

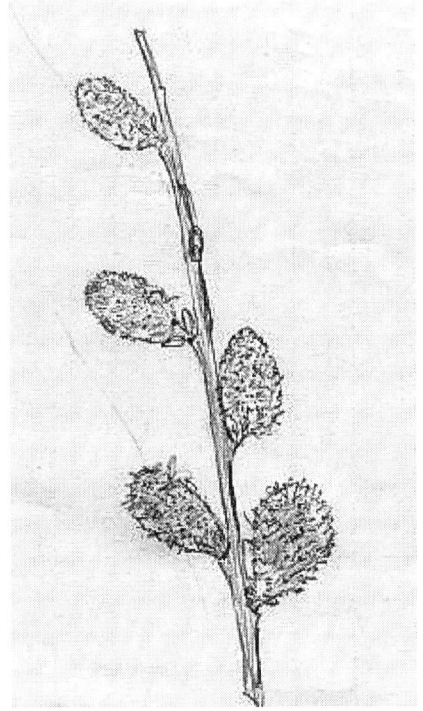

Pussy willow.

On the roadside, where we walked daily, there were only two ways to go - up or down, or if you prefer - north or south. Up took us through delightful mixed woodland - as an adult I discovered that in summer, these woods were full of warblers and other migrant birds - to another clearing in the woodland, locally known as Blarbay, and where the stream here, the Allt Beochlich tumbled under a stone bridge.

Loch Aweside.

We often hung over this to watch the dipper in his smart brown and white plumage bobbing up and down on a stone or disappearing completely into the water in search of food. In springtime the roadside banks were thick with primroses, but also interesting mosses and liverworts, which later, as a student, I collected for microscopic study and identification.

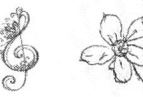

Going south along the road the scene was rather different, for here, in parts, the Forestry Commission had been active in planting conifers, not yet big enough to be too tall and overpowering. Planting was still in progress here over a wide area. In damp ground near the loch, they had also planted some Balsam poplars, whose buds and young leaves in spring exuded a divine perfume fit to die for. Once we took a few twigs home with us to Glasgow and after a time in water we discovered that they had sprouted roots. Sadly we had nowhere to plant them, but my Aunt Jeannie took them to plant in the Mansewood garden. By the Blarghour burn we often saw a grey wagtail resplendent in grey, black and yellow and the heron sometimes stood downstream, waiting for fish.

My parents and the Crawfords became good friends and they often spent their evenings together in front of the log fire. My father, not normally given to such frivolities, was finally persuaded to join in with sessions at Chinese checkers. There was often music too, my mother on her violin and Mrs C. or myself at the piano.

The hall at Sonachan was the scene of local gatherings and I once attended a dance here, where people came from a wide area. Not just the youth, but children, the middle-aged, and the grandparents. The older people chatted and caught up with the news and watched the young folk energetically enjoying their Highland reels and Gay Gordons.

In that same hall, on a night of mixed entertainment, I went on to the platform to play a couple of accompaniments to my mother's violin solos, which I think she chose because of their relatively simple accompaniments. At any rate, I got through them without any wrong notes and we were rewarded by polite applause. Thus, on one single night I had made both my musical debut and my 'final appearance'. Not many can boast of such an achievement!

During one stay at the Festive season, Mary was despatched on foot to the next farm community with a New Year gift. She asked me to come for company and on the way there told me of the two sisters we were to call on. Receiving any bit of news or local gossip one usually said "fancy!" and the other one "mercy!". An unlikely tale I thought, but once there it proved to be true and I was hard pressed not to giggle, even when I was given my first under age drink – a small glass of port.

Over the years, while at Loch Awe, there were occasional visits to Inveraray, the white-washed town on the shores of Loch Fyne. It had once been a busy place during the seasonal herring boom, but now its quayside was largely deserted. It had of course over the years seen many arrivals and departures of Clyde steamers. Now it was also the stance for the familiar green, red, and cream buses of the MacBrayne company, which had a monopoly over much of the West Highlands. The town or much of it was rebuilt in the 18th century, after the earlier town was badly destroyed by civil war and by the great Montrose when he had dared to foray into Campbell territory. The sea frontage forms the cross of a T, with the main street running up at right angles from it. Once I was older, my father was anxious to tell me of the parish church here, divided into two, so that both Gaelic and English services could be held at the same time, before the steady decline in the Gaelic-speaking populace.

There were numerous shops on the Main Street, including the one where I was measured up for my teenage kilt, again in the McDonald tartan, in spite of the ragging I had got a few years earlier at Blarghour, for coming to Campbell country in such a tartan. The reason for that initial choice was because the Hutchisons are a sept of the McDonalds. It was a lovely shop full of tartans and tweeds, travelling rugs, kilts, sporrans, dirks, quaichs, horn spoons and much else.

The frontage of the town, quite imposing in its modest way, included the Argyll Arms, from where there were views across to the folly of Duniquach on its high hill, and to the left to the grounds of the Argyll dukes and their fancy castle, a modern 18th century extension to the original very old one. The Episcopalian church with its fine tower was the place of worship for the Campbell dukes. Father, engaging a man working at its entrance one day in conversation, was told, "Aye, they swing the reek at services here." On a later occasion, while staying further down the loch he had taken his fishing gear up to a small loch in the hills. Once there for a time, a man had appeared and told him that the fishing was private. Father said – "And who may I ask are you?" To which he got the unexpected and haughty reply, "I am Chamberlain to the Duke of Argyll." A very important personage was the Duke!

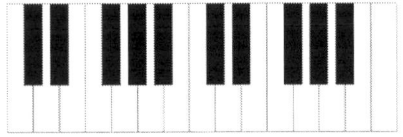

In the late summer of 1940 the Battle of Britain was fought out in the skies over southern England and the Channel by valiant young men in their Spitfire fighters. As Churchill so beautifully said of this time – "Never have so many owed so much to so few". A turning point was hoped for, but German raids over London intensified by September and October and the famous London Blitz, the most severe, came in December. Tremendous destruction was inflicted on its citizens and properties, and with so many resulting fires that it has been described as the second Great Fire of London. The RAF retaliated over some of Germany's cities such as Hamburg. On our side, Coventry's beautiful cathedral was largely destroyed and the cities of Birmingham, Liverpool, Hull, Cardiff, Swansea, and Southampton all took their share of destruction. Through the news bulletins, I was old enough now to grasp some of the horrors of war.

Princess Elizabeth and Princess Margaret Rose were sent to Windsor but the King and Queen refused to leave London and they were often photographed visiting bombed areas, the King always, it seemed, in his naval uniform. When Buckingham Palace itself was bombed, it was said that the Queen was quite glad in a way, because she felt that she could now look the EastEnders in the eye.

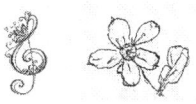

At the height of the Battle of Britain, I had arrived for school in Glasgow and was enrolled at the Glasgow High School for Girls. At that time it sat high above Sauchiehall St. in the Garnethill district of the city. It was a steep climb up, after dismounting from the yellow tram at Charing Cross. The old Glasgow trams all had a broad band of colour below their upper deck, roughly denoting the area that they served. There were blue trams, green trams, white trams, and red trams. These last I had been more familiar with at Giffnock. All of course carried the city's Coat of Arms on the side. The Coat of Arms denotes some of the objects tied up with the story, possibly mythical, of the patron saint, St Mungo, of which I remember little. My mother used to point it out to me with its tree, its bell, its fish, and the ring and the city motto 'Let Glasgow Flourish'. Now from Hyndland a yellow tram would bring me along passed the Kelvingrove Museum and Art Gallery, and the Kelvin Hall, a huge red sandstone building erected in the Twenties as an exhibition centre and circus venue. During the war it became an important factory for the manufacture of barrage balloons. These by now were a familiar sight in the city skies, designed to deter low-flying enemy aircraft.

Near the school was the Beatson Cancer Hospital and the famous Art Nouveau Glasgow School of Art, Charles Rennie Mackintosh's masterpiece. He also designed the Hill House at Helensburgh, now in National Trust hands and a less well-known mansion, Windyhill, at Kilmacolm. He famously collaborated with Kate Cranston, the daughter of a Glasgow tea-merchant and stalwart supporter of the Temperance movement, to design her well-known 'Willow Tea Room'. The link to willow was, of course, because the 'Sauch' of Sauchiehall Street means willow in Scots.

Apart from my second evacuation to Buchlyvie after the Clydebank Blitz, school was at Garnethill now for several years. Here I started to play hockey which I loved, and also went to swimming sessions at the Hillhead Baths. Having expressed a desire not to play tennis, this surprisingly was sanctioned and instead I got an afternoon off – a clever move on my part! The head mistress was the sainted Mrs. Flora Tebb and the teachers, as at any school, were a mixed bag. Our history mistress succeeded with her teaching methods to turn me off the subject completely; alas in later life I discovered that I had a natural interest in the subject but little time to study it. The German teacher was possibly my favourite, with the result that I enjoyed her lessons and managed, in learning about Germany, to detach it completely in my mind from the Nazi regime and the hated Führer.

My classmates were very different to the village children I had mixed with at Buchlyvie, and came from business and professional families. One was the daughter of a medical professor, another's father was Professor of Divinity. Of my special friends one came from a farming family in Lanarkshire, another had a father in business in the city, and one had recently lost her Dad, killed on active service with the RAF. Her mother was going through a period of intense grief and dabbling in Spiritualism. Another of my classmates was the daughter of the Jewish sculptor, Benno Schotz. A few forms above me was the sister of Stanley Baxter who was to become the much-loved comedian. At that time he was still attending the Boy's High and in his brown school uniform.

My classes now introduced me to Shakespeare and some of the major English writers and poets, but one area of study was Greek mythology. Much was made of this for some reason. My father was more than a little sceptical, because of my young age and in any case most of it I have long forgotten. The Art room was colourful, but messy and I was much offended by being told that I could draw quite well but spoiled it completely with paints or crayons. One day, I either fell far short of expectations, or was perhaps rather rebellious – I don't remember – but my punishment was being put alone into a corner cupboard. Well, not quite alone, for I soon discovered that I had a companion suspended from a shelf by a hook, a very real but ghostly white skeleton. If the teacher expected it to scare me, she was foiled, and I emerged eventually without comment and calmly carried on at my desk as if nothing had happened. I hope she was disappointed!

Music was pretty boring, for it consisted largely of singing in the doh-ray-me scale and I never was one to relish singing. I could sing in tune, but could produce no volume. Perhaps I was like the singer that my father used to tell me about whose efforts were once described in Glasgow parlance "You couldnae hear her behind a caur (tram) ticket". There was pretty well no attempt to encourage musical appreciation, except for a couple of visits to orchestral concerts. One such concert included Stravinsky's "The Rite of Spring" and some of us giggled our way through it! Such are the mistakes made in education of the very young, as was the visit to a theatre performance of a French play – possibly Molière, and in French. I was lost!

A big improvement came when for the music class our parents had to purchase a recorder, really an ancient medieval instrument which was enjoying a revival in the 20th century as an instrument for children. I did enjoy this and we learned from proper staff music. I was having private piano lessons at the time but my ability in reading music meant that I always wanted just to play something straight off. Result – little practice and no perfection. My music teacher lived in the next door flat and doubtless might have heard some of my attempts. Instead of repeated practice of scales and chords and the current study pieces, I would drum out popular melodies from Ivor Novello's "Glamourous Night" or "The Dancing Years", Romberg's "Desert Song", and "The Student Prince", and the tunes of Jerome Kern, Irving Berlin and other popular composers from cheap sheet music that my mother bought for me.

School uniform was strictly enforced, pale blue jumpers allowed in winter, otherwise blue shirts and school ties worn with navy gym slips, school blazers, navy nap coats in the winter months and velour hats or in summer the even more hated panama ones, both with a ribbon of school colours.

Also strictly enforced was Morning Assembly, with readings, prayer and hymns. We seemed to be forever having "Let All the World in Every Corner Sing" and I was never an enthusiastic singer. At these gatherings the Prefects were seated up on the platform, which can't have been a very comfortable spot for them, in full view of the rest of the school. One time the daughter of the medical Professor smuggled a guinea pig into Assembly, causing giggles and much wandering of attention.

CLYDEBANK BLITZ

By 1941 the convoys of merchant ships carryings goods to Britain were being severely attacked by German U-boats and there was now war both in Greece and North Africa. President Roosevelt could not actively engage his country in the war because of negative public opinion, but he finally came up with his Lend-Lease plan, where the US would supply military equipment to the UK, not to be paid for while the war was in progress. Finally, he had this passed in Congress. And Churchill famously said in one of his speeches, "Give us the tools and we will finish the job."

On the home front, garden railings, gates and other metal, even pots and pans in some places, were taken for the war effort, to bolster the supply of metals necessary for the manufacture of weapons.

At home the railings all along the streets of Hyndland had been removed and there was now an underground shelter among the lime trees on our road, a shelter that was soon to be in use.

The night of 13/14th of March brought the enemy attack on Clydeside. The Clyde was, of course, vastly important for ship building and auxiliary industries. That night the sound of sirens sent us and our neighbours down to the shelter, my mother waiting long enough to fill a vacuum flask and grab some food. During the next few hours we could hear aircraft overhead, anti-aircraft fire, and the sound of exploding bombs. Bombs were dropped in various places that night, but the chief target was Clydebank, home of the famous John Brown's Shipyard and of Admiralty oil-storage yards. The shipyard and others mercifully received only minor damage but the oil-storage depot took a direct hit, also the nearby Yoker distillery. Gas mains were burst, causing huge fires. There were around 1,000 fatalities at

Clydebank that night, many more injuries and street after street of tenements reduced to rubble. The famous landmark of Singer's factory with its huge clock was only slightly damaged. It was here that my paternal grandfather had once worked as a mechanic.

This was all taking place a mere four miles from us. We were lucky, but as we surfaced in the morning after the nine-hour bombardment, it was to find all our windows smashed and the street full of debris. The nearest bomb had been less than half mile from us at the bottom end of Hyndland and Daddy soon learned that one of his pupils had been killed there.

The brave folk of Clydebank have often been praised, for they carried on at their work even if they had lost their homes and possessions. Many were billeted out in the surrounding Stirlingshire and Dunbartonshire countryside, and had to endure longer, more difficult journeys to and from work each day.

In spite of the broken windows and rubbish I think I was packed off to school that morning as usual. My father went to work, where he too found broken windows and minor damage, and my mother, like so many other housewives, was faced with the clearing up and arranging to have overworked tradesmen to board up and eventually replace the windows.

Street sweepers were soon on duty, clearing the streets although some children were anxious to procure precious pieces of shrapnel. I did this myself after later raids. There were further bombings over Glasgow and surrounding districts and we became used to the wail of the sirens. Sometimes the warnings were of short duration and I once sat one out, grappling with homework, under the sturdy oak dining room table which in happier times could be extended to seat twelve people very comfortably. It also served occasionally as a ping-pong table! Greenock suffered most in the raids of May 5th - 7th 1941 and the last one over Glasgow itself was not until March 1943.

Our school suffered considerable damage and twice we had emergency schooling at our playing field pavilion at Kirklee and in the church hall of the Hillhead Baptist Church, next door to the Baths.

By now there was a steely determination among all sections of the population that we were all part of the fight against evil. Everybody pulled together in a remarkable way regardless of class, background or education. We all had a common foe and a common aim.

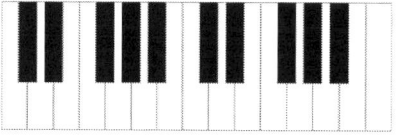

Rationing was accepted with resignation, but it was the poor housewife who was forced to be resourceful in cooking meals with limited supplies. The system began early in 1940 with bacon, butter and sugar rationing and more restrictions were introduced later. Meat appeared to be rationed by a price limit, so the cheaper cuts became popular. Offal was often on the menu in some form or other – liver, kidney, tripe, sweetbreads, pigs trotters and I remember my mother once securing a sheep's head, I think to make broth. It was split in two and spent a day or so soaking in water, teeth and all, to extract excess blood! Precious minced beef was padded out with rice or macaroni to make it go further and Mummy laboriously mixed the 2oz butter portion per person with margarine to make the latter more acceptable. The disgusting Spam and dried egg was imported from the USA. Dried egg was a godsend when the ration was of one fresh egg per person per week. The National Loaf, an unattractive colour, was introduced and a points system which allowed the housewife to purchase other items of food. Sausages contained lots of soya flour. The limit on cheese, I think, was 2oz per person per week. Lord Woolton, the Minister for Food, encouraged the cooking of a pie containing root vegetables instead of meat and it took his name. Carrots became a new constituent of cakes and the public were told they would help them to see in the dark! Oranges and bananas became unavailable after a while.

Ration books were issued in the name of new born babies and my mother one day heard the local grocer saying to a new grandmother, "Well, I hope Baby enjoys his bacon." Housewives more often than not had to stand in queues when shopping for their groceries and word swiftly flew around that certain items were on sale in certain shops. Queues became part of life, whether at the shops, the cinemas, the stations, the taxi ranks. The story was told of someone joining a shop queue and asking those already there what was on offer. She received the reply —"We'll find out when we get there."

My mother's Canadian relations were occasionally able to send a food parcel with tinned fruit, chocolate, sweets, tinned meat and salmon. The latter was hoarded jealously until, as a special treat, it was made into a salmon pie with cereal or potato to bulk it up. Once or twice my Aunt Chris's stepson, who had a managerial post in the fishing industry, had a box sent to us from Grimsby, with an assortment of smoked and fresh fish, which of course was shared with friends. From the local fishmonger Mummy occasionally procured a solid, square lump of salted ling, which had to be thoroughly soaked before cooking, to extract as much salt as possible. Strangely I rather liked it.

Visits to Arran or Loch Awe always allowed us to return home with fresh eggs, some of which would then be preserved in a large earthenware crock with Isinglass, a clear sticky substance made from the air bladders of certain fish. Some people swore the eggs took on a fishy flavour, but they were still much valued and would keep in the crock for a few months. I'm not sure that the purchase of eggs in this way was strictly legal, for once a teacher friend of the family had his car stopped by inspectors on his way back from the countryside and his boot searched! In spite of everything of course a black market did exist and the Spiv was born.

Any excess fruit gleaned from the gardens of friends or relations or indeed the wild brambles from the hedgerows, were carefully bottled in large glass Kilner jars in the days when almost no one would have heard of a freezer. When there was no fruit, the frequent milk puddings had to be supplemented with jam or soaked raisins.

Petrol had been rationed since the outbreak of war, road signs removed or blocked out, and the black-out strictly enforced. Orientating oneself in a dark street was often not easy and once my mother and I, returning from the cinema, and taking what we thought was a straight line across to the opposite pavement, landed slap-bang into one of the trees in the street, where the air-raid shelter lay.

The coupons system was introduced for clothing in the summer of 1941 and the Utility clothing introduced, using the minimum of material. Men's trousers ceased to have turn-ups and skirts became shorter. Socks and stockings were darned and darned again, and elbows patched. For me, I had to endure coats and skirts with big hems so that they could be let down as I grew. A family friend laughingly told of how she had shortened the legs of her husband's pyjamas so that she could patch the 'seat' and saying that, if the war went on too long, he might be going to bed in shorts! Mummy split sheets down the middle and resewed them with the worn parts on the outside. Lots of folk received hand-me-downs, as I did with my cousin Ian's pyjamas and shirts, the latter were perfect for carefree Arran holidays and for a few years I went to bed in boys' pyjamas. Even worn jerseys were now carefully unpicked, the wool rewound and knitted into something else. It was indeed a time of 'Make Do and Mend'. The coupons system for clothing meant that people had to be content with only an occasional new coat, dress, or suit.

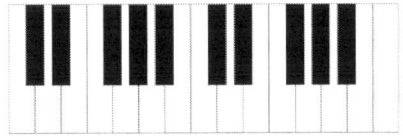

WAR

After the Clydeside raids of 1941, the tentacles of war were spreading ever further and before summer arrived there was fighting in Yugoslavia, Greece and North Africa. The Germans invaded Crete and on the eastern front they invaded Russia. The news bulletins at times were grim and with news of huge losses in the Atlantic because of Nazi U-boat activity. HMS Hood was sunk by the Bismarck and it in turn sunk by the Royal Navy. Revenge, grimly appreciated by the population at large! In Russia, the Nazis carried out terror on the Jewish population, herding thousands into the forests to dig their own graves before shooting them. Much of this was not known until much later.

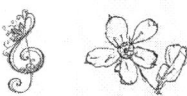

Before the end of the year, the Japanese were flexing their muscles in the Pacific, hoping to extend their influence in the area. Finally they overran Hong Kong, the Dutch East Indies and the Philippines. The 7th of December saw their fierce and devastating attack on U.S. ships at Pearl Harbour in Honolulu. Immediately, both the USA and Britain declared war on Japan and a few days later Germany declared war on the USA. Our two countries were at last Allies with two dangerous enemies to face.

My brother Andrew had been home on embarkation leave and had sailed to the Far East. David was already serving with the Royal Artillery on Gibraltar, a strategically important base, guarding the entrance to the Mediterranean. His letters home carried interesting stamps and told stories of the high-jinks of the Barbary Apes on the Rock.

David.

The Japanese were making steady, indeed rapid progress towards over-powering Malaya, where Andrew had been posted, and their air force sank two British warships patrolling the waters off the east of Malaya, the HMS Prince of Wales and HMS Repulse. By December 1941 British troops were steadily withdrawing southwards in Malaya, and on February the 15th 1942 Singapore fell to the Japs in one of the worst defeats of the war. We knew nothing of Andrew's fate until some considerable time later my parents received a War Office communication informing them that their son had been posted 'missing'.

By this time I was back at the school in Buchlyvie, having been 're-evacuated' by personal arrangement between the Walkers and my parents, who had received a scare with the Clydeside bombings. The schoolhouse was now home to two other Glasgow girls, older than me and both at the senior school in Balfron. They occupied my old bedroom, while I was given a much more luxurious one, thickly carpeted and with lovely green curtains and eiderdown. It overlooked the back garden and I was awakened in the mornings by the cockerel and hens at a nearby cottage, crowing and clucking to the morning sun, a sound I have loved all my life. The older girl had had her piano brought from Glasgow and she was already a good pianist. Her show piece was Sinding's "Rustle of Spring" which rather dazzled me. I was never asked to play on her piano and I was much too shy to ask, but at least there was more music in the house.

I was back with my former classmates as we studied for the forthcoming Qualifying Exam in June 1942. After that there would be no more village school for me. My last year was happy and my days were filled much as they had been before, except that we were all that little bit older now and looking for a bit more excitement. Some of that came in the form of trying our hand at smoking, boys and girls both. We knew the different kinds of cigarettes – Players, Goldflake, Capstan, Woodbine. I know I pinched a few from the sideboard at the schoolhouse and others no doubt would have been procured in similar fashion. We indulged our craze in odd quiet corners of the village, away, we hoped from detection. It was a craze that soon palled for me, although some of us continued smoking cinnamon sticks for a while until supplies must have run out in the local shop! Sexual matters came to the surface in conversation, inevitably, and there were veiled references to pens and inkwells and suchlike.

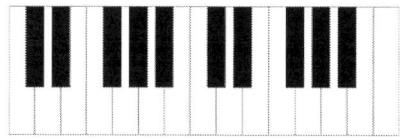

So by Autumn 1942 it was back to the school high above Sauchiehall Street, but this time to the senior school, where I joined the girls I already knew.

My parents still had no word of Andrew and they must have been very anxious and fearful. My mother set about immersing herself in other interests to help keep up her spirits. Music became her salvation. Having played the violin in her youth but giving it up for family life, she decided to try again, setting out to find a professional teacher, and buying a better violin. Music lessons and lots of practice became a big part of her life.

One day a strange postcard arrived from Andrew, confirming that he was a P.O.W. and at least at the time of writing was still alive. The postcard however only allowed him to tick certain boxes – e.g. I am well, or I send love to . . . . At least it brought some hope.

The music continued. I was a beneficiary of Mummy's progress and was introduced to music new to me. She joined forces with a teacher friend of my father who was an accomplished pianist and two teachers from Hyndland school itself who played violin and viola. Musical evenings in the house became regular and finally she even joined the school orchestra.

On her own, her solo repertoire included such much loved favourites as the Meditation from "Thais", the Intermezzo from "Cavalliere Rusticana", Elgar's "Salut d'Amour", and Beethoven's Romance No 2. Occasionally she would take me to an orchestral concert given by the then Scottish Orchestra under its New Zealand conductor Warwick Braithwaite. His immediate predecessor had been the famous Barbirolli. This orchestra, based in Glasgow, became the S.N.O. in 1950 and later still the R.S.N.O., as it is today. Concerts were held, of course in the large St. Andrew's Halls, sadly burned out in later years, but Mummy chose to go on a Sunday afternoon to their performances in Green's Playhouse. This was a huge cinema, seating over four thousand people but was used for other events as well. Sitting in its plush seats I was introduced to serious classical music and was dazzled by the brass section and solo performers on piano and violin. I remember watching the young Polish violinist Ida Haendel perform Mendelssohn's Violin Concerto and at another concert was blown away by the huge chords which override the opening melody of Tchaikovsky's Piano Concerto No. 1. Soon the overtures to 'Oberon', 'The Force of Destiny' and 'The Thieving Magpie', some of Grieg's melodies and the ballet music of Tchaikovsky became firm favourites.

Another of Mummy's distractions was the cinema and she often slipped off in an afternoon to one of the three picture houses within reasonable walking distance from home, including the much-loved Grosvenor on Byres Road. During school holidays and sometimes on an evening I would accompany her. She seemed to enjoy Westerns; I was more attracted to Romance. Some of the big names of the time were Clark Gable, Bette Davis, Katherine Hepburn, John Wayne, Irene Dunne (I had quite a crush on her for a time) James Mason, Humphrey Bogart, Stewart Grainger. Bud Abbot, and Lou Costello, along with the Marx Brothers, provided comedy. There were also the Tarzan films and the wonderful Fred Astaire and Ginger Rogers. I had reached the stage of pinning up photographs of my favourites on my bedroom wall. In an exclusively girls school there were rival camps "madly in love" with either James Mason or Stewart Grainger, myself in the latter camp until, when a bit older, Spencer Tracy ousted him!

It was a time when the cinema was King and Glasgow like other cities had many. Glasgow people long had a reputation for knowing how to enjoy themselves, reflected in the many dance halls and theatres. In the first half of the 20th century Glasgow at one time could boast of fifteen theatres and close on one hundred cinemas.

I was taken occasionally to the theatre too as I grew up, to Peter Pan I remember when I was quite small, and once to the ballet, and much later to a musical show based on Grieg's life and music. Every Christmas we went to a pantomime, usually I think at the Alhambra, or possibly the Pavilion or the Kings. Even my serious-minded father enjoyed the chorus girls and the Principal Boy with, as he put it, "a fine ankle". And he laughed heartily at the comedians, especially if there were slap-stick scenes of Glasgow drunks. On reflection, this was surprising, as he was not in favour of alcohol and seldom partook. None was ever present in the household during my childhood.

My mother's family had also been brought up to scorn it. The story was often recalled of my grandfather's bottle of whisky, which had been won in a raffle perhaps. Grandma had opened it in his absence and poured it down the sink! Even at Christmas dinner the strongest beverage on offer was Ginger Wine. There had been a strong Temperance movement as my parents grew up and Daddy would later recount to me stories of the 'Band of Hope', an organisation usually attached to churches and where the young were entertained with tea and buns, and a magic-lantern show, then invited to sign 'the Pledge' that they would forego alcohol. Such events had been called 'Bursts' because the paper bags in which they had received their buns, when empty, had been blown up and then burst to make a satisfactory noise. He remembered open air meetings too at Bridgeton Cross and the occasional summer outing to one of the parks. Even in my childhood Temperance hotels were relatively common, often rather dull-looking places. No self-respecting woman would have been seen in a public house at that time.

But Glasgow was also a cultural centre, taking great pride in its Art Galleries and Museum, the St Andrews Halls and its very fine Mitchell Library. The library had first been founded on a bequest by Stephen Mitchell, a tobacco manufacturer. It was housed in more than one location until it found its final home in the handsome building near Charing Cross and opened in 1911. Father sometimes went there to read and study. The city's ancient Cathedral and lots of fine Victorian architecture were duly celebrated.

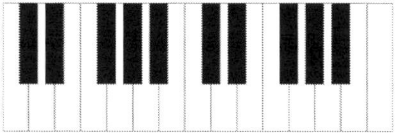

GLASGOW

The Kelvingrove museum and Art Galleries was a place I was taken to regularly by my father, combining a Saturday or Sunday afternoon walk with some education on the side. The imposing red sandstone building was designed by Milner Allan in an elaborate Spanish baroque style and was opened in time for the 1901 International Exhibition held here in the park. It has a magnificent entrance hall and imposing staircase to its upper floor. There was plenty to see and learn but much of it, as a youngster I found a little wearisome, although I did like the stuffed animals and birds, knights in armour, an Egyptian Mummy, and a section with many model ships. Kelvingrove had a wonderful collection of paintings by many famous artists – Rubens, Van Dyke, Monet, and many more, but I was too young for that.

Glasgow University.

We walked home through the park which to one side is overlocked by fine Victorian terraces built by Sir James Paxton. On the other side lie the buildings of Glasgow University, which would become my Alma Mater in a few years' time. Its Gothic-style buildings, designed by Gilbert Scott sit high above the park, the tall filigree spire dominating the skyline. Passing through the park we always had to pause at the statue of Lord Kelvin (1824 – 1907) the famous physicist who had been a Professor here. Dr Green, an old friend of Daddy's, had been an assistant to Kelvin as a young man. It was a tenuous link but one that seemed important to my father. He often visited Dr Green, now that we lived in the same neighbourhood as he did and they would be closeted together in the study of the old house discussing advances in physics and science in general, no doubt. After all, Rutherford had split the Atom in 1932 and the first nuclear chain reaction had been successful in the USA. Radar was already with us, and much else was happening in the field of physics. Mrs Green was musical and sometimes accompanied Mummy on the piano, and occasionally they were joined by son George on his violin too. They tackled more difficult pieces together and I listened and learned.

After Sunday morning service in the red sandstone parish church, we often went for an afternoon walk to the Glasgow Botanic Gardens. In the cold winter months, we would head straight for the Kibble Palace, an imposing structure and one of the country's largest glasshouses. At the entrance area, there was a large pond with waterlilies and gold fish and a wide walking area with seats, huge Camellias in different colours and numerous Victorian sculptures in white marble, nude figures which I looked at but pretended not to! The Kibble Palace had first been erected in Mr John Kibble's estate at Coulport on Loch Long. He later loaned it and finally gifted it to the City of Glasgow.

There were temperate sections and also tropical areas, the steamy heat welcome for a little if it was chilly outdoors. Here palm trees, bananas, tree ferns, and spice plants flourished. An orchid house with its many types gave only a hint of the variety within this one huge family of plants. There were cacti and insectivorous plants to be admired, huge vulgar flowers of Hippeastrum or delicate more modest ferns and climbers up to the upper-most panes. Different temperature areas were divided by glass and doors and by one of those doors – I can see it yet - I fell in love with Crown of Thorns a plant from Madagascar, Euphorbia splendens, fleshy, thorny and with pretty red flowers. It was over forty years later that I next saw it in a friend's house. But its prickly nature meant that it was not safe to take a cutting!

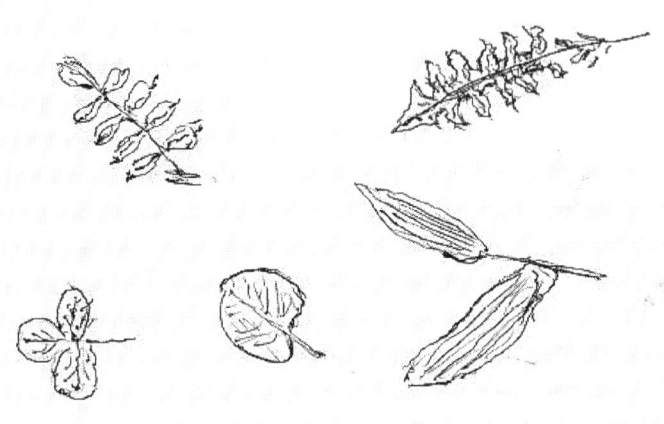

In summer the parkland had flower beds, green lawns and leafy walks down by the River Kelvin, where I first started to identify different trees, as many I could, and at the garden entrance there was a rock garden. Mummy often said poor old Glasgow has to maintain all this, and its art galleries out of city finances, unlike Edinburgh which enjoyed state support for similar facilities! Just opposite the main gate lay the BBC buildings, which had once been St. Margaret's College, part of the University, and for women students in early days. My mother had studied here for her degree.

We walked home along the spacious, tree-lined Great Western Road, the main thoroughfare westwards out of the city. We passed several elegant terraces in different architectural styles, most definitely designed for gra-

cious living for the wealthy. They rejoiced in names equally varied –
Grosvenor Terrace, a grand Italianate affair, long ago converted into the
Reo Stakis Grosvenor Hotel, then Kew Terrace, Belhaven Terrace, Great
Western Terrace, this last a masterpiece of Alexander Greek Thompson's.
Hyndland almost rubbed shoulders with this area but by comparison was
somewhat downmarket!

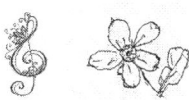

In the better weather of Spring, not having a garden to escape to, we
liked to get out of town on a Saturday afternoon. By train from Hyndland
Station or by bus along the Great Western Road, our destination was perhaps most often to Milngavie and district. Here were the Mugdock
reservoirs, holding points for the city's water supplies which are piped all
the way from Loch Katrine in the Trossachs. It was lovely soft water and
required little soap to produce a fine lather, a decided advantage when soap
was rationed during the war. It was often said that this soft water was one
factor in the high incidence of tooth decay in the young, but other areas
might well be envious of its purity. Beyond the reservoirs lay the woodland
of Mugdock, rich in wild flowers in springtime and the site of Mugdock
Castle, a former seat of the Montrose family, now in ruins. Walking further
we passed Craigallion loch with its ducks and swans and then out into an
area of rough grassland and moorland where skylarks trilled in the blue
sky, and lapwings tumbled and dived in their crazy display flight, wings
drumming. It was hard to believe that this was a mere four miles or so, as
the crow flies, from the city. The haunting calls of the curlew added to the
feeling that we were truly out in the wilds. We often picnicked here from
the goodies that had been carried in a haversack by Daddy.

Carbeth loch and view to Drumgoyne and the Campsies.

Beyond lay Carbeth where there was a colony of weekend huts and cha-lets in different styles, all proudly maintained and painted up by city weekenders who escaped here for a taste of simple, country living, away from busy streets and tenements. I was more than a little envious of some of the colourful huts and quite fancied living here for a little. Beyond lay yet another loch, Carbeth, and views to the Campsie Fells. Another part of the Milngavie area had a boisterous rookery where the cacophony of sound in early Spring thrilled me, and all my life I have loved the sound of a rookery with the birds busy in their twiggy tree-top nests.

West of Bearsden we found and explored another area for walks, to-wards Faifley and north of Clydebank, and in the shadow of the Kilpatrick Hills. Now aged twelve, my interest in plants was expanding. On one stretch of moorland we discovered masses of blaeberry (or whortleberry) in fruit in autumn and we picked enough for my mother to make blaeberry and apple pie. This plant is a close relation to the American blueberry, nowadays widely available on supermarket shelves, and treasured for its health-giving properties. In this same area there were some post Great War

smallholdings which had been built under a scheme to give returning soldiers homes and to allow them to cultivate a few acres. Here I was
introduced to a sweet-smelling field of beans in full flower and thick with
bees, a scene I have remembered all my life, not having known before what
beautiful flowers the humble field bean had. And near here on a shady
roadside I found the very strange blooms of Cuckoo-pint, each green
spathe enclosing the phallic like spadix. My little notebook of this time
records that I could see the 'little purple thing that sticks up'.

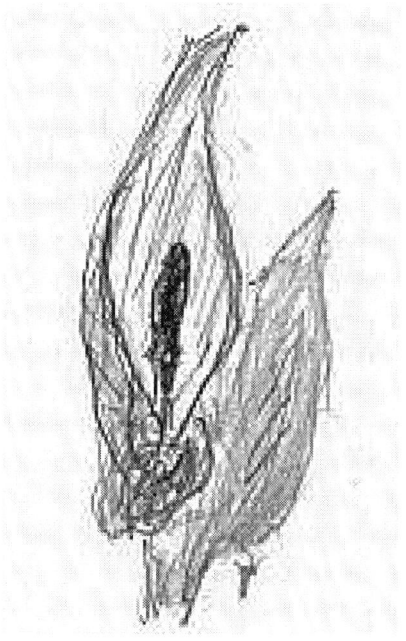

Cuckoo-pint.

It was through a chance meeting here with some anglers carrying their
rods and baskets that my father got into conversation with them, and found
out that there was a fishing club up in the Kilpatrick Hills. With true west
coast friendliness they asked him if he would like to become a member.
And forthwith he did, within a very short time. The club members fished a
couple of lochs, Cochno Loch and the Jaw. Of course the Kilpatrick Hills
are scattered with other small lochs. This was private ground in these days,

but I believe that now there are many footpaths open to the rambler, and that the Cochno Estate is an outlier of Glasgow University. Mummy and I sometimes accompanied my father here on his fishing trips, enjoying the walk up to the moorland, through a bluebell wood before we reached the open ground where whaups called, and skylarks reached towards the heavens in trilling song.

The fishers here had a little bothy where they could rest and shelter and infuse tea from the kettle which was kept hot on a small stove. There were rough seats fashioned from turf sods. My mother swore that the anglers didn't bother to empty the teapot, but just kept adding more tea leaves and boiling water! Certainly, it was a strong brew, drunk from billycans and enamel mugs. Primitive but friendly!

Most of the men who fished here were from the Clyde shipyards. With continuing losses of both merchant and naval vessels in the Atlantic, torpedoed by the German U-boats, the work was constant in the shipyards to build more and more vessels, as quickly as possible. These men must have given their all, overstretched and weary. This fishing club would have given them peace and relaxation, and restored a sense of normality when nothing was normal. They were so friendly and down-to-earth that my father gained much from his association with them.

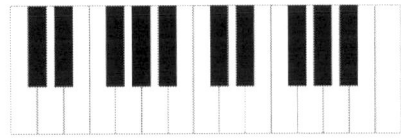

During the war, the river Clyde and its estuary became immensely important, not only for its industrial output so necessary for the war effort, but also because it was further away from possible attack by the Luftwaffe than our other big ports. It assumed a major role in receiving goods and military equipment from the USA and elsewhere, but also as the chief port for the arrival and departure of thousands of troops. At times the lower reaches of the Clyde were crowded with merchant ships, destroyers, cruisers, air craft carriers, and of course the famous troopships, Cunard's 'Queen Mary' and 'Queen Elizabeth', the latter launched by the Queen only in 1940 and taken over immediately on completion as a troopship.

There were booms across the Clyde to deter enemy attack and the Tail of the Bank as it was popularly known, that stretch of water between Greenock on one shore and the sandbank running down from Dumbarton on the opposite shore, was the scene of great naval activity. It was from here that troopships would anchor prior to embarking military personnel to various theatres of war or after bringing American troops here in huge numbers in the build-up to the invasion of Normandy in June 1944. My two brothers departed from here to their posts overseas, although we didn't know that at the time. It was from here too that there were arrivals and departures of Churchill, Roosevelt, Stalin, Generals, Ambassadors, and the King himself. To deal with all the activity on the Clyde, a new harbour was built in the Gareloch and much of the famous Mulberry harbours used in the D-Day landings were assembled here. Naturally I was unaware of all this at the time, but people who lived further down the river must have viewed much of this activity and drawn their own conclusions. But the population during the war obeyed the orders not to gossip and possibly pass information into the wrong hands. "Careless talk costs lives" and

"Mums the word" were well-known phrases, a variation being, "Be like Dad, and keep Mum."

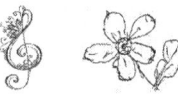

What I was very much aware of as a schoolgirl was that the streets of Glasgow were awash with servicemen and women here on short leave. Uniforms were everywhere and seemed as common as 'civvies' and they were of course of great interest to me - Norwegian sailors, Free-French, Canadians, US sailors with their pork-pie hats, Poles, British sailors, soldiers and airmen, and of course the Yanks. Often while waiting for my homeward tram after school, I would see the G.I.s meeting up outside the flamboyant Art Nouveau Beresford Hotel with local girls, perhaps hopeful of receiving gifts of the coveted nylons, the men possibly looking for rather more. As the saying went at the time, they were "over-paid, over-sexed, and over here". One joke of the time was about the latest fashion in knickers – "one Yank and they're off!" The uniforms in such variety were everywhere, in the shops and restaurants, on the trams, in the cinema queues, the taxi ranks, and at the stations.

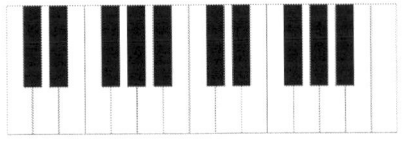

ARRAN (AGAIN)

During these years, the holidays to Arran continued but even here there were signs of war. I think the railway stations still had their posters advertising such varied things as Bisto, Beechams Pills, Pears Soap, Waverley Pens, Creamola custard, Camp Coffee, and Sunny Jim's 'Force' cereal, but the names of stations, like road signs, had been removed.

My father knew the railway line down to Ardrossan well, and he was always anxious to point out the famous Coates factory at Paisley. The cotton industry had reached its height during the 19th century, including the manufacture of the famous Paisley shawls, known the world over. Now after a steady decline Paisley manufactured mainly cotton thread. My father's interest in all this stemmed from his boyhood in Bridgeton with its then thriving cotton industry. Many Ayrshire towns too had a past history in cotton, woollen goods, and lace-making. Near the coast, Daddy was equally anxious to tell me about the explosives factory at Ardeer, established here in 1873 by the Swedish chemist Alfred Nobel whose fortune later established the famous Nobel prizes.

Crossing to Arran in wartime, we often saw naval vessels, cruisers, destroyers, and submarines. They all had precedence over our small passenger steamer and after orders from the bridge to the engine-room, and with much bell-ringing, we might swiftly alter course. Passengers often rushed to the deck to see what we were avoiding. The result as often as not, with such delays and late, and crowded trains, was that the steamer would be late arriving at Brodick pier.

The islanders became used to waiting long past normal arrival times to receive goods or guests. A holiday friend of my brothers wrote at that time in my autograph book, with some hyperbole, of course –

'What matters,

Tho Arran's peaks be lost in grey,

And gone the blue from Brodick bay,

The Rosa burn be wild with spate,

The old 'Glen Sannox's three hours late.'

There were booms guarding the entrance to Lamlash bay as this too was a small naval base, and the steamer had to go round the outer side of Holy Isle before heading for Whiting Bay. There were often naval ships at anchor here too while crews had brief time onshore. This same bay has given safe harbourage to ships since early times and it was here the Vikings brought their longships when ravaging western Scotland. King Haakon of Norway assembled his fleet here in 1263, before embarking for the Ayrshire coast and his defeat at the Battle of Largs. During the Great War too it had been a small naval base. Now in modern times the bay is attractive to many yachts and pleasure craft. In World War II, although Arran remained a haven of peace to holiday makers, the Naval presence made a modest increase to the population. The Marine Hotel at Lamlash housed naval personnel and Altnacorvie, later the home of the Holiday Fellowship was where WRENS were billeted. Brodick's Auchrannie Hotel, later to become the island's top hotel and holiday complex was also requisitioned by the Navy.

The south end with its Escallonia and Fuchsia hedges and small fields of grazing cattle remained unscathed except for the occasional sound of naval gun practice out at sea and the night-time hum of passing air craft from Prestwick airport. At this time it was one of the U.K.'s busiest, handling much of the air transportation of supplies across the Atlantic.

Fuschia

And so it was back to Glenside and the old routine of farm and the beach. This was so much quieter now with the young people of my brothers' generation mostly away in the Services and families broken up. Younger and older were still there enjoying the peace and quiet. On the way to the beach we crossed the old golf course now given over to grazing for the Ayrshire cattle who left their cow pats here and there, horseflies or clegs as we knew them homing in on them. My sandshoes flicked through clovers, ribwort plantains, purple selfheal and the yellow rattles that really did rattle as flower gave way to seed.

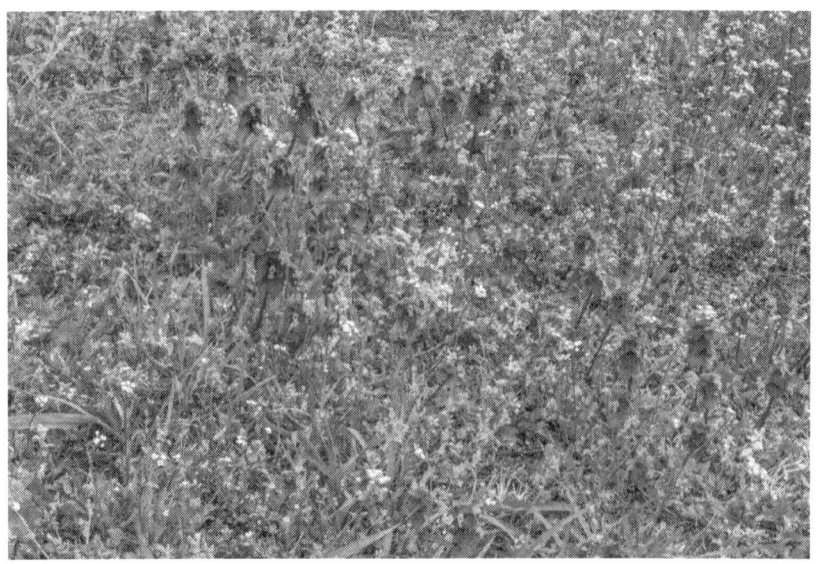

Purple selfheal.

Yellow-rattles.

Seawards, the end of Kintyre seemed close and also the two islands of Sanda_and Sheep Island, which together make up what is affectionately known as the Spoon, for together they look exactly like a large downturned spoon lying on the surface of the water. On a really clear day we could just make out the tip of Northern Ireland. At the entrance to Campbeltown lies Davaar Island with its lighthouse. Sometimes in the shortening days of August my father would walk in the late evening along to Butterhill and point out the different lighthouses each with its unique code of lights flashing on and off – Davaar, Ailsa Craig, Turnberry, and Ayr. Daddy had for a short time during the Great War, before serving on the Continent, been in charge of an artillery base at the Cloch Lighthouse and he knew the Clyde coast and its lighthouses well.

Agrimony.

Down the cliff path where spikes of agrimony grew, over the dyke and across the short turf to the shore I could now identify the delicate pink centaury flowers, the palest pink stars of English stonecrop and the blue button heads of sheep's bit scabious and the magenta clumps of bloody cranesbill. Describing this plant it was quite permissible to let the swear-word fall from my lips as often as I liked!

Sheep's bit scabious.

Bloody cranesbill.

The obligatory swim was an almost daily habit. Now I had gone far beyond the sandcastle stage. Instead I wandered along the beach poking
about and admiring the different shells washed up on the tide line, periwin-
kles, small delicate pink tellins, striped whelks, the occasional long blue
razor shell and little scallops. Occasionally there would be a beautiful
prickly sea urchin washed up. Little collections of these shells were treasured for a time.

145

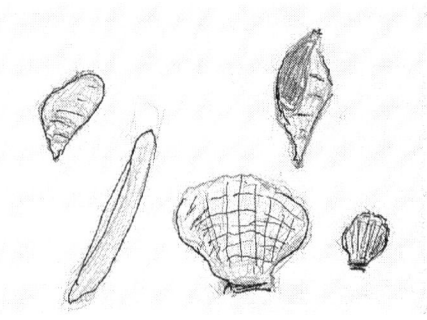

Seashells.

By the summers of '43 and '44 however I was more keen to make a collection of wild flowers and they were abundant and varied at a time when
fields and roadsides were never sprayed with insecticides or weed-killers.
These horrors came in the future, to the detriment of many natural habitats.
The roadside grassy banks were rich with birds-foot trefoil, tufted vetch,
bell heather, orchids, and thyme. Sometimes I wandered off on my own
down sloping ground behind the farm which led passed cultivated fields,
where by July, the potato crop would be in flower in whites and mauves.
The sandy ground here suited both the potatoes and the strips of carrots
with their feathery sweet-smelling leaves.

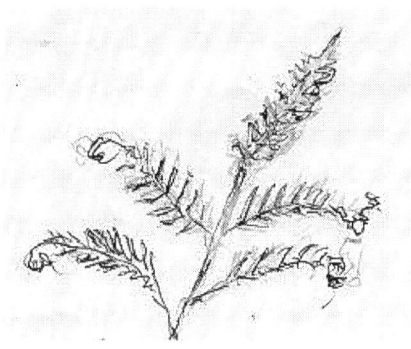

Tufted vetch.

Arran had had its own early potato breeder in a local man – Donald
'Tattie' McKelvie, who gained recognition between the wars for breeding
many varieties such as Arran Banner, Arran Chief and Arran Pilot. Some

146

are still available today. My path down by the potato field meant that before I reached the grassy haugh by the burn I had to negotiate two gates in the form of old iron bedsteads, held in position with wire or rope. Old bed ends were commonly seen on the island, either as gates or to make a barrier in a gappy hedge. If there were proper gates they were of the old wooden five-barred type quiet to open and not scaring the animals or birds as the modern metal ones often do.

The hedgerows here were thick with honeysuckle as indeed they were along many of the roadsides. A most beautiful flower with a heavenly perfume in the evening, or after rain. It remains to this day in my 'Top Ten'. Also in this category is the Butterfly orchid, and down here in the grassland by the burn I knew I would find lots of their creamy spikes exuding an unforgettable perfume. I could pick a little bunch of these without compunction to decorate the kitchen table.

Butterfly orchid.

The cornfield which I passed had lots of flowering 'weeds' before the advent of nasty weed-killers – corn pansies, fumitory, sun spurge and scarlet pimpernel. Two of the cornfield weeds I sometimes picked to put on my table-top jug or jam jar are now quite rare, the sunny yellow corn marigold and the large hempnettle with purple and pale yellow blooms. Down in the burn where monkey flower and valerian grew in clumps I sometimes paddled, and on one occasion I remember going into a deeper brown pool in my birthday suit. The sun dried me in no time. This was a spot I well knew was isolated!

Sun spurge.

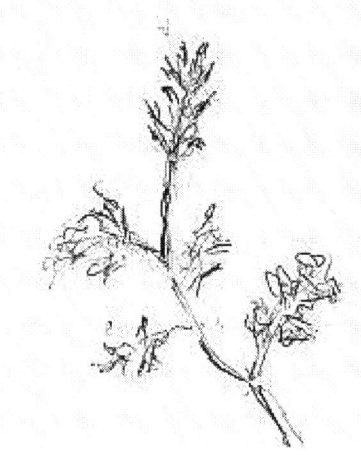

Fumitory.

Scarlet pimpernel.

Corn marigold.

One excursion oft repeated over the years was the walk over the moorland road to Auchareoch farm, roughly three miles there and three miles back. This was too far for a small child but as I grew older I accompanied my parents. There were two motives for this tramp. One, for the sheer enjoyment of being out in the wilds among the heather, where red grouse sometimes called "go-back, go-back" before rising on whirring wings. From the lower ground curlews voiced their haunting calls and the smell of heather wafted on the breeze. Our second motive especially in the war time years was to obtain fresh-laid eggs, homemade butter and the thick oatcake bannocks which my father loved.

These acres of moorland were all forested back in the 60s but we knew them long before the road was open, the moorland wide with lots of meadow pipits in song-flight and with views towards the source of the Kilmory water up near Auchaleffan, the neighbouring sheep farm to Auchareoch. What lovely sounding names both of them! From the Gaelic, Auchareoch might be translated as the grey or brindled field but the other name again 'a field' but of what kind I've never found an explanation.

Here and there along the rough track there were bare patches at the edge of the moor where sheep must have lain up at night, leaving their droppings and scraps of wool which clung to the woody heather stems. By August the bell heather was followed by the ling, the true heather, and in damp patches cross-leaved heath flowered in pale pink. The big areas of bog asphodel told by their yellow spikes that this was a place where one's shoes were almost sure to get wet, but a beautiful plant, even past flowering, when it glowed orange over the moor.

Bog asphodel.

Before we crossed the wooden bridge below the Auchareoch steading we could smell the peat smoke on the air and hear the first barking of the collie dogs. Crossing the grassy slope up by the dry-stone dyke we arrived at the back door and were welcomed by widowed Mrs Walker, who kept house here for three bachelor shepherds, her two brothers, and her only son.

Up by the dyke to Auchareoch.

The big black kettle hanging on the swee above the range would soon be on the boil and cups of tea would be served with freshly baked scones and a boiled egg if we wished it. The welcome was warm as was the kitchen, especially on warm days. The window looking out over the garden was never open; perhaps it was jammed for all I know. With the tea, the chat would begin. The men were for most out on the hill or around the steading but one might join in for a little. In spite of the remoteness of the farm and with no telephone, they were remarkably well informed about both local and world news. The wireless and the "Glasgow Herald" were their links to the outside world. Angus was the brother we saw most often, a gentle, kindly man, and so well-informed about wildlife. He often accompanied us a short distance on our return walk. Father especially enjoyed his company, so much so, that he had once walked with him the five miles or so from the steading over moorland to Lamlash, driving sheep that were headed for the steamer and the sales.

Mrs Walker herself rarely seemed to sit down and often carried on with her baking of scones and thick oatmeal bannocks. She scorned shop-bought bread, scones or jam, and much else which she described as "trash".

My future sister-in-law, on one visit, asked for her scone recipe. She chuckled and said she didn't have one and then described how she measured things in handfuls, pickles, pinches and splashes – of milk, or buttermilk! Often a glass of the latter was offered to Daddy which he liked a lot. I simply loathed it. The bannocks were made on the girdle (Scots for griddle), hanging on the swee and finished off against the front of the fire while propped up on a flat iron. On our departure, some means of payment was carried out by my father in front of the big dresser, adorned with a miscellany of crockery, tins, and much else. The money was stored in a large tin here!

One time I remember we were asked to stay on for a meal with them, when we all sat round the table, the men having removed their cloth caps and hung them on the backs of their chairs. The meal was of freshly-caught brown trout which Angus had taken from the waters of the nearby stream of Allt Nan-sluice. Fried in oatmeal and served with floury potatoes and lots of butter, it was a meal fit for a king.

The folks here lived a simple life yet they gave the impression that they were content with their lot. Miles from a shop and with no vans, Willie, the other brother was the 'traveller', crossing the moor to Shannochie for supplies, or by bus to Whiting Bay. The garden produced basics like leeks and kale in winter, rhubarb and bush fruit to make jam in summer. Anything that was purchased in bulk, including coal, sheep-dip, netting and other necessities for the farm were dumped at their road-end near Glenside, and they had to handle it themselves by horse and cart up the three miles of rough road. Roll-on roll-off ferries didn't come until the 60s and in these days coal was brought to the island by 'puffers', the little working boats on the Clyde, made famous by Neil Munro in his Para Handy tales. No lorries could trundle off the ferries as they do now. Puffers came into little quays round the island, such as Brodick, Whiting Bay, Blackwaterfoot, and Corrie. Into the 1960s I remember often seeing the 'Roman' at Brodick.

Life at Auchareoch was simple, but hard; animals had to be fed and peats cut, paraffin lamps filled. There was cold running water in the scullery but dishes were washed in hot water from the kettle. I don't know if there was a W.C. somewhere, but nobody ever seemed to 'go' anywhere, and we never got beyond the kitchen door, except, after a bathroom was installed in later years, my mother was taken upstairs to be shown this marvel of modernity. On the farm there was the constant round of milking the cow, herding the sheep, lambing, dipping, clipping and the driving of animals over the hill to the sales.

The stone fank at Auchareoch.

I remember on one of our many visits here, they were busy at the dipping in the big stone fank behind the farm and I was an eager observer, as the sheep were immersed, head and all into the foul smelling liquid, then watching them swim along a channel before release into another pen, vigorously shaking themselves to be rid of surplus liquid.

So on our departure from Auchareoch each time we would have bannocks and butter, eggs, and a few blocks of peat for us to burn and enjoy the smell of peat reek. The neighbours to the other side of the farm at Smuraig, I don't think even had a road to them at all, and burned peat exclusively. That area was a mystery to me but I liked its name.

However long the holiday lasted – two whole months sometimes - like all good things, it had to end. The last few days were spoiled with cleaning and packing the trunks, but to the end there were visits to the shore, up onto the moorland, and an evening walk to the road-end. Then goodbyes to all my favourite animals and the bus to Whiting Bay for the steamer. If the weather was good we would stand on deck, watching the island recede from us, myself certainly feeling very sad.

Once off the gangway there was usually an undignified scramble to get to the train to secure seats, if possible forward towards the engine. On arrival at the city that meant a shorter walk. The trains were often overcrowded, with people standing in the compartments of the corridorless carriages. At Glasgow, St. Enoch's Station – long gone - we hurried passed the still hissing engine at rest on the big silvery buffers, the driver and fireman chatting, and out to the inevitable taxi queue. With the good nature and friendliness of the Glaswegians, sometimes a shared taxi was secured if our destinations were to the same area.

GLASGOW

It was always a shock to the system to return to the city after the freedom and fresh air on Arran, but Hyndland was relatively peaceful, and in a few days it was back to the usual routine.

By this time I had acquired my longed-for bicycle. On its arrival, Daddy had wheeled it across to the empty school on a Saturday afternoon where in the open quadrangle at the centre of the school I learned to ride it, away from any observers. This same school had long since been shown to me and other family members with great pride. I was already familiar with my father's office and the adjoining one of his secretary. We had toured the classrooms, the labs, the gyms, and the self-contained 'flat' where girls from the B stream had lessons in domestic science. This especially fascinated me. In another year or two this would be the school where I would finish my education, after my father's retiral and here I was to enjoy the happiest of my school days, apart from the village ones at Buchlyvie.

Having secured my bike, I was soon to make new friends, finding other youngsters in the district also haring around on bicycles at the weekends or on summer evenings. Then a gang of seven or eight of us stayed out until the last possible moments. The wartime streets here were quiet, so occasionally we ventured as far as Byres Road, indulging in coffee or soft drinks in a café there, or we bicycled along Great Western Road to Bingham's boating pond and, sharing our pocket money, hired a couple of rowing boats.

With this group of youngsters and as we got older, I was gradually learning. Occasionally there would be a pairing off. My first 'boyfriend' came from a mixed marriage between Jew and Christian, and one of the girls lived alone with her father, her mother having gone off with another man. Such things had not been heard of in our family.

Rosalind and her bike.

This was also a time of parties among my Girls' High schoolmates at houses far and wide. My recollection of these events is that most of the games seemed to end in an excuse for necking. The numbers of boys and girls were always exactly matched, the boys chosen from the High School, Kelvinside Academy or other boys' schools. We were all quite good at the kissing, emulating the film stars of the day, whose romantic films invariably ended in a clinch!

The war continued, with its horrors and losses. Newspapers and wireless bulletins gave constant news. War raged on in the Soviet Union but eventually the Germans met their match in the bravery of the Russian people. The battle of Stalingrad was protracted, but the Nazis finally surrendered it in 1943. Churchill and Stalin met at Casablanca and agreed that the bombing of German industrial centres should be intensified. By Spring joint bombing raids by the RAF and the USAF (well settled now in Britain), became intense. The chief targets were in the industrial heartland of the Ruhr valley. Night after night, day after day it continued. The bombing of the dams, later made famous by the film "The Dambusters" and Eric Coates' wonderful music, followed with the loss of huge amounts of water essential to the German industrial machine.

Partly replacing the screen heroes and heroines, the generals became much admired – Monty in his beret, who commanded the 8th Army troops to their victory at El Alamein. Auchinleck, Wavell, Patton, and eventually Eisenhower (Ike) were household names. Photos of some of them were pinned up on my wall.

As I grew older and while the war raged on, my father continued my unofficial education with outings to various parts of the city, where he showed me places and told me bits of old history. He was immensely proud of being a Glaswegian, and by the time I had reached my later teens the city wasn't only my home, but of course, the centre of the universe!

We visited Glasgow Cathedral, the only Scottish one apart from Kirkwall's to have survived the Reformation. It was built in early Gothic style and has a fine vaulted crypt. Provand's Lordship, the oldest house in the city, was also visited. It dates from the 15th century, now a museum. I found it cramped, dark, and rather overwhelming.

I learned a little of Glasgow's history from my father as we walked around. Its early trade in tobacco and cotton from the Americas had built up its wealth and the so-called Tobacco Lords had lived in fine mansion houses in the area called the Merchant City, between the town centre and the river where goods had arrived. The famous Broomielaw by the Clyde was celebrated in more recent times as the departure point for steamers going 'doon the water'. Of the old buildings, of course little was left, but Glassford Street was named after one of the Tobacco Lords, and Virginia Street's name speaks for itself.

When we went to visit Glasgow Green, the historical site of the Fair held during the second half of July, we were close to the centre of the cotton industry in Bridgeton, where Daddy had been brought up. Much of it had been demolished and upgraded so he couldn't take me to see where he was brought up. He was one of the five surviving children out of seven, and he was told that at his birth they didn't have much hope of him surviving. But survive he did and lived a long healthy life. The one scar he bore was the bone damage done to his legs, due to rickets. In Victorian times in crowded cities, with little exposure to sunshine as many as nine out of ten children might suffer from rickets.

At one time Bridgeton had been the site of several cotton factories. Singer, the huge sewing machine operation was also here before moving out to Clydebank, its buildings to become a local landmark. Grandfather Hutchison had worked here in his time. Templetons, the famous carpet manufacturer was also in Bridgeton. The face of Templetons lies to one side of Glasgow Green, the elaborate building imitating the Doge's Palace in Venice and looking very unlike a factory. It was opened during my father's childhood and continued to flourish, and even during the years of the Depression it was still expanding. In 1937, the Coronation carpets for the Westminster Abbey crowning of George VI were manufactured here.

Bridgeton Cross, with its famous meeting place of yore under the 'umbrella', the Tolbooth and Glasgow Cross and more were all visited, areas I had never been to and to some would never return.

On the west side of the city we visited the Fossil Grove in Victoria Park, where fossilised tree trunks are preserved in situ. A few years later this was re-visited when I was a student. Our Professor was an expert in the world of fossils and to visit here was obligatory!

To the south side with my father and mother there was Pollock Estate to explore with its lovely parkland bordering the White Cart River, and a handsome Adam mansion house. This was familiar territory to my mother, she having been brought up in the Shawlands area and I think school or Sunday school outings were made to the estate. The lands of which Pollock formed a part had been owned by the Maxwells of Caerlaverock in the 14th century. The last baron died childless and the estate had passed to one William Stirling of Kier. The 20th century landlord, Sir John Stirling Maxwell, combined these two family names and I often remember my mother referring to him by name. He had planted the fine Lime Avenue to celebrate his 21st birthday in 1888. In modern times of course, the estate has become the home of the famous Burrell Collection gifted to the city of Glasgow.

Before moving to Mansewood, Mother had been brought up in Regent Place in Shawlands and received all her schooling at the Academy there, followed in due course by all her younger siblings. As a bright pupil she was eventually chosen to become a pupil teacher. Under this scheme some older pupils became assistants to the established teachers, thus using their youthful talent to share the burden of teaching the huge classes of the time. Indeed as a young teacher herself, she had to cope with a class of nearly sixty children!

Mother went on to Glasgow University to become an early woman graduate. Her youngest sister Lillian followed her here much later, graduating in English and History. Glasgow University was one of the earliest universities to accept women as equals with men. The St. Margaret's College for women was absorbed into the university but Mother had attended some classes here in the building by the Botanic Gardens before it became the centre for the BBC.

She often talked of her student days, before gaining her MA degree in the subjects of English, Latin, German, Mathematics, Logic and Moral Philosophy.

And so she became a teacher, and as luck would have it, received a post at her old school. And there, by that time the mathematics master was my father. His budding romance was furthered by Uncle George Wishart, also a teacher who took him under his wing and finally asked him to come and meet his sister, my grandmother, and the family at Mansewood.

My parents were married at the end of June 1913 and set off to honeymoon in Germany and Switzerland. The following year, 1914, they returned to both these countries and indeed only made it safely home on practically the eve of the outbreak of war.

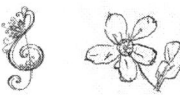

Right through the war years our visits to Grandma were regular. She was gradually ailing and finally took to her bed with recurring bouts of bronchitis as well as on-going arthritis. She lived long enough to see the war over and my two brothers safely back in Scotland.

To visit her we went from the West End by subway from Hillhead to Bridge St. The Glasgow subway, with its orange coloured trains was quite an institution and a speedy way to reach some parts of the city, its twin tunnels allowing trains to circle the extent of the system in clockwise or anti-clockwise directions constantly during the day and evening. The city council tried to improve its image by calling it the Underground but in truth it still remained affectionately known as the subway.

The rest of our journey was by tram, but first we had to walk a short distance to the tram stop in Eglinton Street. This was where I saw a little of the seamier side of Glasgow. If the afternoon was fine there would be numerous women 'hinging oot' of the thrown up sash windows of the tenements, elbows on windowsills, watching the world go by and getting, perhaps some sunshine, for there were railway lines and goods yards on the opposite side of the street, and no towering tenements to block the sun. Close to the Gorbals here, sometimes there would be a woman pushing a pram full of clothes, on her way to the 'steamie', as the communal wash-house was known. Occasionally I had to share a seat on the tramcar with a fat and smelly (they always seemed to be smelly) woman with her baby wrapped close to her in a woollen blanket. Quite possibly there was no money for a pram. The menfolk however found the money to frequent the pubs. On a Saturday, around here they were busy and the mixed smells of sawdust, whisky, and beer issuing from their doors I found disgusting. There could be vomit on the pavement and men weaving an unsteady path along the street. I never saw any violence however, and the drunks were either good-natured or most often completely indifferent. Once, my father encountered a drunk on a tramcar who was not only very talkative but in-sisted on parting with some of his money to him in spite of several polite refusals. For peace, in the end he had to accept, and the stranger seemed strangely gratified and friendly.

Leaving this side of Glasgow behind, the tram rattled on, taking us to the quiet and decorous district of Mansewood.

As 1943 progressed, with the war in Russia, and increased Allied bombing raids over Germany, the news bulletins still reported the losses of ships and men in the Atlantic and the loss of aircraft over Germany. By summer Allied troops had landed in Italy and very slowly but steadily forged their way northwards, their aim – Rome. Many of the Italians had no real wish to go on fighting and more or less gave up, leaving the fighting to the Nazis. By October, the Italian Government deposed Musso-lini and held him under arrest. They declared war on Germany and would now support Allied troops – up to a point!

In the Pacific, the Americans were making progress in capturing one is-land after another, until they were close enough to be able to launch air attacks on the Japanese mainland. This progress came with colossal loss of life.

By the end of the year the Big Three, Churchill, Roosevelt, and Stalin, met at Teheran for yet another conference and all the papers carried photographs of the three men sitting together. It was here that plans were made for the final invasion of Europe. Stalin was pushing for speed, but Germany had to be considerably weakened before an invasion had any hope of success. So into 1944, bombing raids were intensified over the industrial heartland of Germany. At this same conference Roosevelt and possibly Churchill too were anxious about Stalin's plans for a post-war Europe, and suspected that he was aiming to extend communism to areas of Europe as they were liberated. A 'whiff' of the Cold War to come.

Into 1944 the Allied bombing raids were intensified, hitting Germany's industrial heartland of the Ruhr Valley. But at great cost on both sides. The French resistance movement became more active and daring but the Nazis, although weakened, continued to transport Jews to the gas chambers, and their bombing raids on Britain continued. The Allies resorted to many ploys of deception to mislead the Germans into believing that an invasion was being planned for the Calais area. The code-breakers of Bletchley Park knew their deception was working, and that the Germans were strengthening their defences in that area.

So on June 6th 1944, U.S., Canadian, and British troops made their landings on the beaches of Normandy. The news bulletins now became riveting and in spite of the colossal loss of life, we at home began to believe that this might be the beginning of the end. But still the enemy had a nasty surprise up its sleeve in the form of the flying bomb – the Doodlebug or the VI, which terrified people in London and the South-East. Its frightening, approaching whine would suddenly cut out and nobody knew where it was going to land and explode. It caused many casualties. We had first-hand accounts of this scary development from our relations in London.

In France, the Allies made slow progress, for a time advancing little. Even the battle for Caen was protracted. By this time I had secured a large map of Europe through the U.S. National Geographical Magazine, sent to me by my Californian cousin George. It was put up on my bedroom wall. With coloured pins I followed the allied troops' advances. By August, Paris was liberated by Free French troops and General de Gaulle returned to his capital city. By September it was the turn of Brussels, but the ambitious parachute attack at Arnhem in Holland was not a success and there were many men injured, killed, and captured here.

On the Eastern Front however the Soviet troops were making significant advances, eventually crossing onto German soil.

By the end of January 1945 they broke through the Polish border near Auschwitz and it was they who discovered the emaciated, starving survivors, the Nazis having fled but leaving plenty evidence of the holocaust horrors. Dreadful pictures appeared in the British press of these survivors.

By February there were pictures of the Big Three at yet another conference, this time at Yalta. The general public still believed that the three men were united in aim but the truth was that Stalin now had his own agenda, his sights set on extending Communist rule into the nations that the Soviets were liberating. Nevertheless, U.S. and British air forces were still aiding Stalin's advance by continued bombing by day and night, notably about this time causing the dreadful destruction of the city of Dresden.

A Germany now almost certain to be defeated, still successfully launched the V2 rocket bombs against England.

From now, in the Spring months of March and April events quickened in Europe and each day seemed to bring fresh news, broadcast by the BBC. The coloured pins changed position on my map with remarkable speed. I found it, in a way exciting, but at only fourteen years of age, I'm sure I failed to realise what sacrifice was involved on personal levels, for at home, life seemed quite secure with little chance now of enemy attack so far north. The rationing and food shortages, and make-do-and-mend of course continued as before.

By April U.S. troops had reached the concentration camp of Buchenwald and the British liberated Belsen. In the same month everybody was stunned by the news of President Roosevelt's death, he having not so long before secured a 4th term of office. The new President was Harry Truman, his face soon familiar to all in the British and worldwide press and news reels.

Hitler refused to surrender even when the Allies arrived in Berlin. He took to his bunker and on April 28th committed suicide along with his lover, Eva Braun. Admiral Dönitz now became the new Chancellor and fighting continued for another few days.

By early May the Germans finally capitulated on the night of the 6th and Churchill declared May 8th as VE Day. Parts of the country, notably London, went wild with dancing on the streets; church bells rang and Union Jacks flew. The shipyard sirens on the Clyde thundered out as they traditionally did to bring in the New Year. Hyndland was near enough to some of these yards that the sound of the sirens was quite familiar to us, as they marked the end of shifts. On VE Day there was a bonfire and celebrations at the bottom end of Hyndland and a big gathering of people. My parents and myself did go, but my father was somewhat reluctant, as the war with the Japs had not been won and Andrew was still a P.O.W. somewhere in the jungle of the notorious Thailand-Burma railway line, if indeed, he was still alive.

A great victory had been won in Europe. However, for myself at home I was to suffer a defeat. Towards the end of the school session, the Headmistress summoned me to her office where she told me that she was going to recommend that I should, next session, repeat the 3rd form. On receiving this news my father had other ideas. As an educationist, he didn't much favour the going over of old ground and believed that I would be better to face the challenge of moving on. He had faith in me, I think, and proposed instead that I should return to Hyndland School and enter the 4th form. It appeared seemly that he would soon be retiring and therefore not involved in any accusation of favouritism. In this he did me a lasting favour, for here, at last, I found much happiness in school life and here I was to stay till I completed the 6th form.

During the months of early summer much was still happening in the world. The war in the Far East continued, but plans were in the making for the Allies to invade the Japanese mainland by the end of the year. The Atom bomb was ready to drop if necessary and in Europe plans were in progress for post-war boundaries of the liberated countries and the United Nations Organisation was being set up. A General Election had been called after VE day, and the result for most of our family was not the one they would have wished for. Father was disgusted that Churchill, who had inspired the nation during the war, had so summarily been ousted from power. But of course many had long been hoping for change and perhaps it was, at the time, inevitable. Poor Mr Churchill, though, who came home half-way through the Potsdam Conference being held between the Allied leaders at that time, to receive the election results, didn't return. Mr Attlee now joined the conference as the new Prime Minister.

Father definitely thought that Churchill at least deserved electoral success even if only as a reward for his years of magnificent leadership. There was a heated argument one day between himself and my cousin Douglas who was a fiery young sixteen or seventeen year old socialist at the time. My mother had to stop the volley of angry words, trying to calm the waters between them.

During that summer of 1945 we holidayed again at Kilmorie during July, just the three of us, following much the same routine as always, but anxious about the news on both the world stage and the home front, where all the P.O.W.s held by the Germans had now been repatriated, and the new Labour Government was settling in.

Regarding the Far East there were reports that the Japs intended to ignore the Potsdam Declaration asking them to capitulate or face the war against them intensifying. Intensify it did, with the dropping of the Atom bomb on Hiroshima on August 6th, followed by the second bomb, dropped on Nagasaki three days later. The appalling carnage brought a very quick end to the war when the Japanese surrendered on August 14th/15th. The 15th was my father's birthday but it was not much celebrated for there had been no more of those strange postcards from Andrew for some time, and we still did not know his fate. Seventy years on, we are all dismayed that these bombs were unleashed on Japan and horrified by the consequences. But the Allies have justified it on the grounds of stopping the war and in the end the saving of many more lives.

And it could well have saved my brother's life, for by late August word was received by my parents that indeed he was alive and had been taken to hospital in Rangoon and would be brought home by sea with his surviving comrades. David, who had been stationed in India for several years, got the good news through a nurse he had known in India and who, now nursing at Rangoon, had recognised the family resemblance! Treatment in hospital and the sea voyage home restored a measure of health to Andrew. From ship he wrote home and one day I was thrilled to receive a letter from him, just for me, telling me about him watching flying fish from deck as the ship crossed the Indian Ocean. I took the letter to school and shared it with my friend Lilias from Buchlyvie days and now a classmate at Hyndland again.

After Andrew's homecoming my mother did her best to feed him up for he was covered in boils and sores, and, on doctors orders swallowed yeast tablets at every meal. The psychological scars of life with the Japs in some ways never left him and he never talked of the horrors he had experienced. For many years he certainly hated the Japs, and would never have dreamt of buying anything made in Japan. In a few short weeks he and his sweetheart, June, who had waited faithfully for him during his years of incarceration were married in a registry office, much to my mother's disappointment (the Registry Office, not the wedding). David had to wait a good while longer to be released from army duties in India. He had mixed feelings, glad to be reunited with his family but regretful for having to break the friendship he had formed with some Indians, notably his Parsee batman. Returning servicemen were issued with one suit of clothes for free.

The big chains, like Burtons, who had been manufacturing uniforms during the war, were now churning out civvies for returning troops.

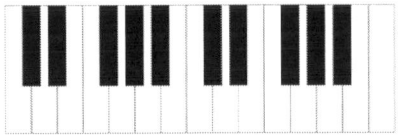

It was now post-war Britain, but also Austerity Britain. The truth was that the country was broke, and now and for many years to come our debts to the U.S.A. had to be re-paid. Much reconstruction work was required to repair or replace damaged properties and infrastructure. A rash of unpre-possessing 'pre-fab' houses appeared as dull grey 'boxes' in many of the open spaces, but which brought a big improvement in living standards for many people, now with hot running water and fitted kitchens, luxuries pre-viously unknown. Furniture was scarce and many a couple setting up home used disguised tea-chests for tables and borrowed anything they could from parents. The furniture on sale, I think, was subject to a coupons system, as clothing continued to be. Coal supplies were needed for industry and the railways, so restrictions were in place. To preserve supplies power-cuts were frequent. Many of these were organised, sometimes with power being cut for several hours a day, but some came at unexpected moments. With the cold winter, they were particularly hard to bear. On one such occasion my mother was painting the kitchen ceiling while perched on steps placed on top of the kitchen table. Trying to descend safely to the floor in the dark she put her foot in the paint tin!

Christmas 1946 and into the New Year, we spent with Aunt Winnie and Uncle Willie in Leicester. My cousin Barrie, kept saying, "we're not going to let that damned Labour Government spoil our Christmas" and on the whole, it didn't. I do remember toasting muffins at the fire in the dark for afternoon tea. My aunt in her endeavours to secure a turkey for Christmas Dinner had taken the precaution of ordering one from three sources. Three were eventually offered!

By the end of 1945 Father had retired from Hyndland School and once again became a lecturer in the Jordanhill College of Education where there was a post-war influx of ex-servicemen and women wishing to enter the teaching profession. My mother continued with her musical interests and I progressed at school – slowly!

Food rationing continued right up to 1954 and for a time was even stricter, with bread rationing for a time. Improvements were gradual, such as the withdrawal of the 'National Loaf' and the introduction of the coveted white bread – the 'pan' loaf, the plain loaf, etc. I remember when Stork margarine reappeared, and oranges and bananas were available in the shops again even if bananas were only supplied at first to the under 18s. Confectionary came off the coupons system along with other gradual improvements. But the black market and Mr Spiv lived on for a while.

There was mounting discontent in the country, especially amongst ex-servicemen. After all we had won the war and things seemed no better, in some ways worse. This discontent was reflected in Tommy Handley's ITMA shows with the arrival of the new character, Mona Lott, whose catch phrase was "It's bein' so cheerful as keeps me going." The Govt. pressed on with its nationalisation of coal, electricity, and the railways, but they also managed to launch the NHS in 1948.

So now I was back in school with boys and girls, male and female teachers and a system that I fully favoured. Many of the teachers were interesting and here I found my all-time favourite in the form of a tall, dark gentleman, Mr Spiers. His easy-going temperament and encouraging approach to the teaching of English delighted me and his classes were always enjoyable. We studied a range of English literature, prose, poetry, and some plays, and homework sometimes involved having to write critiques and analyses of certain passages, as well as the weekly essay.

I loved Chaucer with his quaint 14th century English. For sheer fun I once wrote a parody of one of his Canterbury Tales, describing our French mistress, who was strict, a little old-fashioned, perhaps a hint eccentric. Some of my classmates were chuckling at it when Mr Spiers, arriving for class, asked what was so funny. I owned up to it and he said, "Come on, let's see it." He read it to himself in front of the class, unsuccessfully hiding his amusement. But he was not at all convinced that there wasn't a tale about him. Later on I wrote a parody on Wordsworth's "The Solitary Reaper". That one was about myself and my problems with maths, and made it into print in the school magazine.

One of the teachers was known as Killer Dawson on two counts – some of the girls found him so very attractive, but although exceedingly jovial at times, he was a very strict disciplinarian and didn't hesitate to use the strap if he deemed it necessary. It always lay, fully displayed on the top of his desk as a threat or a deterrent. One master, Mr Cunningham, was known to all as Sly Bacon, others by much worse names. My maths mistress finally encouraged me to maths success, although she did occasionally ask with a smile if my father had not helped with a homework exercise! He almost never did.

6th former with hockey team.

With boys and girls together, one new aspect to my schooldays was having dancing lessons in the big gym. We learned some Scottish dances with reels and strathspeys, but also ballroom dancing and we practised waltzes, the quickstep, foxtrot, and veleta. Some of this was in preparation for the annual Christmas dances, held for senior pupils.

These were occasions to get dressed up and I remember the year I got my first long dress, dance shoes and evening bag. But a few days before the big night I was mortified by developing a crop of teenage spots, which Mummy and I did our best to treat and disguise. I think all went well on the big night. Everybody dressed up and it was a special honour if one of the male teachers, dressed in dinner jacket and black tie, asked you to dance. My enthusiasm for dancing at this time encouraged me to try to teach David some of the basic steps as we glided across the dining room floor together!

At school, I still struggled with maths but enjoyed most of the other subjects except French. However there were Botany lessons from a young

172

lady who was totally uninspiring and I was much disappointed and felt that I was learning little new. My father eventually solved my discontent by buying me a copy of Brimble's Intermediate Botany and I set to, studying it for myself, possibly diverting my efforts away too much from other subjects.

At home I had finally been given a new radio, which sat on my bedside table, so that I could enjoy the kind of music that my parents didn't particularly care for. Late at night if I turned the volume down I was able to enjoy the popular music of the times. The age of the Big Bands had not passed so into my private environment came the music of Geraldo, Ted Heath, Joe Loss, Ambrose and Caroll Gibbons, and memorable tunes like "These Foolish Things", the lovely "Deep Purple" or "Dancing on the Ceiling". Victor Sylvester with his strict-time "Quick-quick-slow" was popular and Edmundo Ros with his rhythmic Latin music.

The radio for family listening was more sober with news bulletins, the Brain's Trust, Sunday gardening programmes, but there was also "Dick Barton – Special Agent", and many a laugh we had with Tommy Handley's much loved ITMA show – never missed. Mother always enjoyed a play, with Father grumbling on the side-lines.

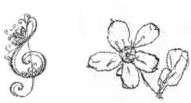

During the mid-40s we had heard about the Andersonian Natural History Society of Glasgow and my parents and myself joined as members, myself possibly becoming the youngest in the society. Indoor meetings were held in the old Glasgow Technical College, while on spring and summer outings we explored the surrounding countryside. The membership included professional people and also enthusiastic amateurs. There seemed to be a bias towards plant life, which pleased me enormously and I was able to learn more about our native flora. I was inspired in that by two very different gentlemen, one John R Lee, already I think in his eighties or near,and author of the "Flora of the Clyde Area". Mr Lee was patient and kindly and very good at pointing out little details of plants in order to make a proper identification. Early on he introduced me to the tiny "wee toon clock" (Moschatel) which I would possibly have overlooked as it skulks under hedges in its greenish garb. Father later bought me a copy of the book and I busily ticked off as many plants as I could find. The second man who inspired me was Richard Prasher, a ganger working on the Ayrshire railway lines. In his day the railway embankments were rich with wild flowers and he seemed to know them all. Not of course that we could study them on a railway embankment, but they were often to be found elsewhere. Mr Prasher, over the years to follow, became a good friend. Soon I was to emulate these two gentlemen in possessing two hallmarks of a field botanist - a good hand lens hung round my neck and a black tin vasculum on my shoulder to keep specimens fresh till we got them home for further study, or to press between sheets of blotting paper to make a personal herbarium. Everywhere we went wild plants were abundant – in woods, fields, roadsides. Sadly I have, over the last forty years and more, seen such abundance steadily diminish. Back then we could not foresee the damage that man and his methods have wreaked on the environment.

Moschatel.

On our society outings we explored the Clyde valley, with its tomato farms and orchards, the Ayrshire coast, including the area where the

Hunterston Nuclear Power Station was later built – spoiling a peaceful spot, rich in wildlife and plants. We botanised in Renfrewshire, on the Campsie Fells, and even at Possil Marsh in the middle of the city, where I first found greater spearwort and tufted loosestrife.

Budding botanist.

During my years at Hyndland school much was happening in the world. Discontent which had been rumbling for years in the colonies of the Empire broke out post-war with India gaining independence but only by being partitioned with Pakistan and with much accompanying violence. After India came Ceylon and Burma. After that the total break-up of the British Empire was underway. The United Nations Organisation was set up, and the Nuremberg Trials were much in the news as senior Nazis went on trial.

There were bright happy moments of course. The family car had been sold and before the third Rover arrived, David bought a small second-hand car and we were able, in spite of continuing petrol rationing until 1950, to have the occasional outing to favourite spots, Loch Lomond and the Trossachs, Loch Ard and Aberfoyle, myself always looking at the plants, and discovering the delicate water lobelia for the first time at Loch Chon. We drove to Loch Katrine, and sometimes through Glen Fruin to Helensburgh. On these outings we either had picnics or a meal in a hotel.

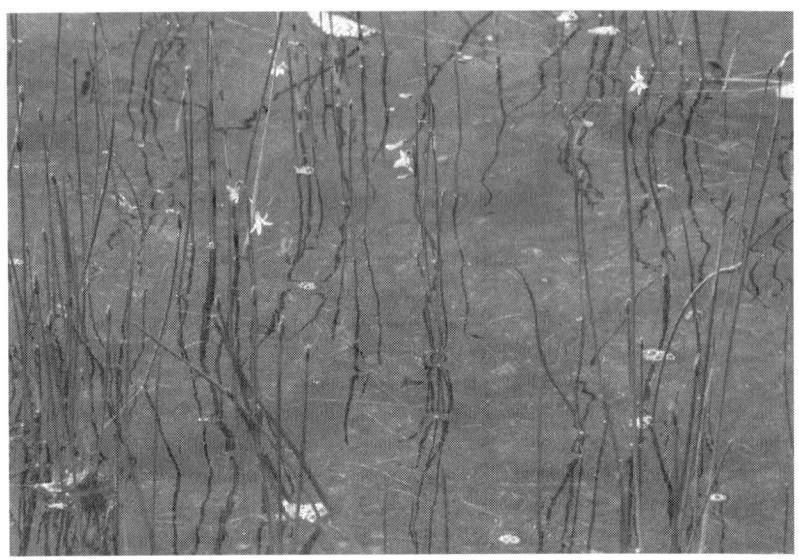

Water lobelia.

The tunes from the musicals "Oklahoma" and "Annie Get Your Gun", were all the rage, and there were interesting films to see such as "Gone With the Wind", "For Whom the Bell Tolls (about the Spanish Civil War), "Henry Vth" and "Pride & Prejudice", both of which starred Laurence Olivier. There were films with a wartime background of course, including "Dangerous Moonlight", about a musical Polish airman and which featured the wonderful "Warsaw Concerto", loved still. And I remember two films with a musical theme – one about Chopin, another about Franz Liszt, the superbly gifted, flamboyant pianist that I couldn't get out of my head for ages.

The whole country got a psychological boost with the engagement and marriage of Princess Elizabeth to the stunningly handsome Prince Philip of Greece. I believe that members of the public donated some of their clothes coupons towards the making of the Princess's lovely wedding dress.

I was busy studying towards my Highers. For a while I flirted with the idea of studying medicine, or even becoming a lawyer! My father thought my talents would serve me well in the Civil Service, but a family friend, whose son was in it put me off that idea. Perhaps I might be a teacher like my parents? No, all these ideas were discarded because of my interest in plant life. So I decided on a degree in horticulture. I was accepted by Reading University, but was still immature and not happy about going so far from home. Prof Braid of the West of Scotland Agricultural College in conversation with my father on an Andersonian outing, suggested that I might go to intermediate level at Glasgow, then go on to Reading. That university agreed to this and would have fast-tracked my degree afterwards. So, in 1948 I left school and after holidaying on Loch Fyneside and at Whiting Bay on Arran, I reached Glasgow University, where both my parents, my Uncle George and Aunt Lillian had all graduated and where my cousin Douglas was now studying in the Faculty of Medicine. Even brother David later found his wife within the walls of this University, so it was rather a special place to all of us.

I settled, very happily, into student life here, and after my two years, forgot about Reading and horticulture and decided to go on to the Honours course in Pure Botany. This proved to be a lucky decision not only because I could now study my first love of plants in depth but it was where a few years later I found my second love, the love of my life. These two loves, often in tandem have given me the greatest happiness of my adult life, but that is another story.

Now, alone and in old age, it is the love of the plant world that remains my inspiration to carry on and where music is often my greatest solace. In writing these memoirs, it has helped me to keep my parents and the rest of my family alive in my heart and allowed me to relive some of a very happy childhood and youth.

The love affair with the Island of Arran did not end here, for in 1953 after a holiday at King's Cross, when I botanised seriously all over the island, Mother and Father moved from Glasgow to settle in Brodick, where they enjoyed their later years and where they once more had a garden to tend.

So this, for me, now became official "home".

Mother still pursued her musical interests and was lucky to make more than one new musical friend. She was also sometimes asked to play the organ at services in the local church.

Mother, aged 93, still playing her violin

My parents finally moved into Montrose House at the end of 1974, where they were well cared for. Father died at Lamlash Hospital in 1976, at the age of 96, my mother carrying on, still interested in everything around her, even taking up painting around the age of 90, when her violin playing was becoming increasingly difficult for her. She saw her 100th, 101st, and 102nd birthdays, still alert and positive and made it to within a month of her 103rd, when she died in Montrose House.

Mother & Father in their Brodick garden.

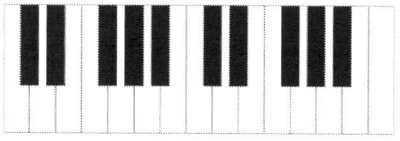

What a desolate place would be a world without a flower

It would be a face without a smile

A feast without a welcome

A J Balfour

In Sweet music is such art

Killing care and grief of heart

Shakespeare

Printed in Great Britain
by Amazon